Preaching for Discipleship

Preparing Homilies for Christian Initiation

MICHAEL E. CONNORS, CSC

LITURGY
TRAINING
PUBLICATIONS

Nihil Obstat
Reverend Mr. Daniel G. Welter, JD
Chancellor
Archdiocese of Chicago
December 5, 2017

Imprimatur
Very Reverend Ronald A. Hicks, DMIN
Vicar General
Archdiocese of Chicago
December 5, 2017

The sample homily used in chapter 4, Homily, "Rite of Acceptance into the Catechumenate and Meeting with Catechumens at the Closing of the Year of Faith," Address of Pope Francis, Vatican Basilica, Saturday, November 23, 2013 © 2013 Libreria Editrice Vaticana. Used with Permission. All rights reserved. The sample homily in chapter 9 © Joseph Ring. Used with permission. All rights reserved. The sample homily used in chapter 10 © Paul Turner. Used with permisssion. All rights recerved.

Excerpts from the English translation of *Rite of Christian Initiation of Adults* © 1985, International Commission on English in the Liturgy Corporation. All rights reserved.

PREACHING FOR DISCIPLESHIP: PREPARING HOMILIES FOR CHRISTIAN INITIATION © 2018 Archdiocese of Chicago: Liturgy Training Publications, 3949 South Racine Avenue, Chicago, IL 60609; 800-933-1800; fax 800-933-7094; e-mail: orders@ltp.org; website: www.LTP.org. All rights reserved.

This book was edited by Kevin Thornton. Víctor R. Pérez was the production editor, Anna Manhart was the designer, and Luis Leal was the production artist.

Cover art: Leonard Porter, *St. Paul Preaching to the Athenians on the Areopagus* 2009, Oil on Linen, 12 x 19 inches. Private Collection, Gallup, NM © Leonard Porter 2009 .

22 21 20 19 18   1 2 3 4 5

Printed in the United States of America.

Library of Congress Control Number: 2018933684

ISBN 978-1-61671-417-8

PDH

Contents

Foreword

Deciding what to preach about is one of the hardest and most important decisions a priest or deacon makes every week. The Lectionary and liturgical texts open up endless possibilities for themes. A good preacher has to decide which one of these is the best for this time and place.

Surprisingly, we preachers don't get much specific direction. On Holy Thursday, the rubrics for the Mass of the Lord's Supper ask us to preach on the institution of the Eucharist, priesthood, and mutual love (*Roman Missal*, Thursday of the Lord's Supper at the Evening Mass, 9). But other liturgies do not carry such explicit directions.

When it comes to preaching at the various steps of initiation, the *Rite of Christian Initiation of Adults* offers even more meager advice. At the Rite of Acceptance, after the readings, we are told, "A homily follows that explains the readings" (63). During celebrations of the Word of God during the period of the catechumenate, "A brief homily that explains and applies the readings should be given" (88).

At the Rite of Election, the bishop or his delegate receives this clue: the homily "should be suited to the actual situation and should address not just the catechumens but the entire community of the faithful, so that all will be encouraged to give good example and to accompany the elect along the path of the paschal mystery" (129). But for the scrutinies, the celebrant explains their meaning "in the light of the Lenten liturgy and of the spiritual journey of the elect" (151, 165, and 172). Really, that's not much to go on.

Instructions for the presentation of the Creed, however, are more explicit: "The celebrant explains in the homily the meaning and importance of the Creed in relation to the teaching that the elect have already received and to the profession of faith that they must make at their baptism and uphold throughout their lives" (159). But the only advice we get at the second presentation is this: "the celebrant in the homily explains the meaning and importance of the Lord's Prayer" (181).

At the Preparation Rites on Holy Saturday, after the readings, "A brief homily follows" (194). OK, but what are we supposed to say?

At the rites of initiation themselves, the RCIA incredibly is silent about the homily, and for the Easter Vigil *The Roman Missal* merely states this: "After the Gospel, the Homily, even if brief, is not to be omitted" (36).

With so little guidance, preachers often take the path of least resistance: they improvise. Or they repeat the homily that they gave the last time they presided for a similar event. Even some bishops repeat the substantial content of their homily for the Rite of Election year after year after year. Well, priests, deacons, and bishops are busy. They have other responsibilities. They have other homilies to prepare. If they can cut a few corners on preaching, they can devote more time to other demands.

This is true not only of adult initiation rites. Many preachers repeat major portions of their homily at every infant Baptism, Confirmation, *quinceañera*, wedding, and funeral. In the life of the priest, these events are repetitive. But in the lives of the faithful, these are once-in-a-lifetime experiences that have taken months of preparation and will be forever remembered. The disconnect between the experiences of the minister and those of the faithful may become painfully evident in a poorly prepared homily.

Preparing to preach takes time. Deciding on the theme is only the start. Constructing the homily requires as much imagination. So does its delivery. However, the hard work of preparation respects the lives of the faithful who are marking important moments of transition in their spiritual lives. These occasions deserve fresh preaching.

The liturgical books do not give much direction on how to do it. But this book does.

Michael E. Connors, CSC, has fostered a lifelong love for the rites of Christian initiation and for the art of preaching. He has absorbed these ministries into his own service, and he is anxious to share the fruits of his work with you.

In these pages, you will meet an experienced priest at home with the People of God. He knows not only his assembled community, but the catechumens as well. He has spent time with both experienced and aspiring members. *It is hard to preach effectively if you do not know the people to whom you are preaching.*

You will also find explanations of the rites of initiation. These rites are unusually complex, and many priests have not had the benefit of extended study on their structure, meaning, and history. It is not completely their fault. Among liturgical rites, these are some of the most difficult to grasp and to celebrate effectively. Helpfully, in this book, before reading pointers for preaching, you will find explanations of the ceremonies. *It is hard to preach effectively if you do not know the ceremony you are celebrating.*

You will also find sample homilies. One of the professional drawbacks of ministry is that we rarely get to hear one another preach. We're all preaching in different locations on the same day at the same time. Furthermore, not all preachers prepare a written text. Consequently, it is hard for them to share their work outside the liturgical moment. Some priests and deacons record their homilies, and these videos and audios provide realistic samples. However, the written word lets readers analyze and study the intrinsic structure and spirit of a homily. Thankfully, this book contains a rich array of sample homilies. The author throws his own work out for your scrutiny, criticism, and acceptance. It takes a confident and charitable preacher to do this. *It is hard to preach effectively if you do not know how others are approaching the task.*

Preaching well requires pastoring well. Those who care about their people will care about their homilies too. The careful preacher will discover something else. The time he spends in preparation will add fuel to his own spiritual life. He will come to a deeper personal acceptance of the Word of God. He will also enrich the lives of his people who hunger for the Word.

Preaching well at the liturgies of initiation will proclaim to all the community the mystery of faith, the call of God, the response of humanity, the growth of community, and the ever-pervading presence of the Body of Christ. It deserves attention. You will find it in this book.

Fr. Paul Turner, STD
Pastor, Cathedral of the
Immaculate Conception
Diocese of Kansas City-St. Joseph, MO

Preface

Not long ago I had the pleasure of reuniting with some old friends over dinner at a local restaurant. A priest, two married women, a widow, and a married man—we have always been a diverse and unlikely group. What brought us together was not a shared interest in bridge, nor the proximity of a shared neighborhood, nor a school, social network, or family ties. What brought the five of us together more than thirty years ago was our work together on the RCIA team of our parish. I was a freshly minted priest just learning how much I didn't yet know. One other member of the team, our leader, had a theology degree and some years as a lay ecclesial minister doing mainly adult faith formation. The others were more or less ordinary but interested lay Catholics, all parents, from different walks of life. At the outset we barely knew one another, but our collaboration over a period of five years of catechumenal ministry bound us together in a way that has sustained at least intermittent contact ever since.

What we shared over those years was more than work—though there was plenty of that! Our experiences went well beyond the many tasks and demands, the challenges, the common moments of good humor and pain. Our attempts to lead others into the fullness of membership in the Church enabled us to encounter the living God. This encounter forged lifelong bonds among us.

We became deep and lasting friends; yet, after all these years and the many varying experiences that have intervened, when we gather it still feels like we are all awed witnesses of something profound, something beyond us, something that seized our minds and hearts and called forth a faith and generosity we had not known in ourselves before.

In a sense, this book has been gestating ever since I left Little Flower Parish in 1989. It feels like the payment of a long overdue debt. Of course, I can never repay the many blessings I received in those years. I recall with gratitude the many people who helped to introduce me to the riches of the RCIA: teachers, formators, supervisors, catechists, the

North American Forum on the Catechumenate, and the Church itself, whose wisdom expressed at the Second Vatican Council gave birth to this phenomenon that is both restoration and creative pastoral expression. Of the many blessings of Vatican II, none has been more formative and more life giving for me personally than the *Rite of Christian Initiation of Adults*. Its vision of Christian faith and Christian community has continued to guide and inspire me through subsequent years of study, pastoral work, and academic engagement, now primarily in the field of homiletics. I seize every opportunity I can to share with my students the treasure we have in the process of initiation, when taken seriously and done well. "For the vision is a witness for the appointed time, a testimony to the end; it will not disappoint. If it delays, wait for it, it will surely come, it will not be late" (Habakkuk 2:3). The vision of the RCIA is still working to renew and reinvigorate the Church; of that, I am still fully convinced. Let us be faithful to the breadth and depth of this vision, resisting liturgical minimalism, resisting the ever-present temptation to truncate, cut corners, and settle for mere indoctrination instead of true, multi-dimensional conversion. Initiation in the pattern of the RCIA is a lot of work, with many moving parts and multiple possible complications. However, it's worth it, because those who come to us hungering for God's life are worth it and Christ himself both prompts their interest and our response. Our reward is no less than the joy which life in the Spirit brings.

This book is written primarily for Catholic liturgical preachers. It springs from the conviction that preaching plays an important and sometimes underappreciated role in the initiation process. Preaching through the rites and seasons of that process can be vital not only for catechumens and those engaged with them as sponsors and catechists, but for the entire parish community who accompany them. Thus, this work's readership will be predominantly priests and deacons, although lay preachers and catechists can also, I hope, read it with interest and find here some inspiration and orientation for their ministries. I hope it may also be of interest to the wider ecumenical homiletic community, from whom I continue to learn so much.

Many people have contributed to making this book possible. I am grateful to Liturgy Training Publications for their constant support and encouragement. I owe special thanks to my ever-patient editor, Kevin Thornton. As well, I thank my brother priests Frs. Paul Turner and Joseph Ring, who contributed homilies included in this book. I am grateful to my department and dean for allowing me to carve out some time to pursue this writing. I am, as always, indebted to Virginia Marten and her family for their generous support of Catholic preaching. Most of all, I am enormously thankful to all those with whom I have been privileged to collaborate, especially at Little Flower Parish, as well as before and since then; I dedicate this work to catechumenal teams everywhere. I want to say to you: what you are doing is vitally important for the Church and vitally important for the lives you hold in your hands. Thank you for all your efforts to share the faith we love with others. May you too have the experience that my friends and I treasure: the discovery of the Risen One walking among us, still appealing, still healing, still reconciling, still seeking out the lost, still routing the darkness with his light, still transforming lives, still turning death into life.

Introduction

I arrived at Little Flower Parish as a newly ordained priest. Flush with enthusiasm, little did I know how much of my education in ministry was still to come. Little Flower was one of those wonderfully, sometimes bewilderingly, active parishes—a community with a strong tradition of lay leadership in every aspect of its life, from liturgy to social engagement to religious education. I was thrown into the usual array of parish activities: I celebrated Masses, preached, heard confessions, buried the dead, witnessed marriages, went to parish council and committee meetings, talked with people who were troubled. For most of these things, I was at least moderately well prepared; for some, like marriage preparation, I was completely unprepared and had no choice but to "learn on the job."

As a seminarian, I had done a "Beginnings and Beyond" institute, sponsored by the North American Forum on the Catechumenate. That workshop, together with an ensuing field placement in RCIA ministry at another local parish, were truly eye-opening, life-changing experiences for me. Here I found the dynamic, evangelical Catholic Christianity for which I longed. So I eagerly joined the RCIA team at Little Flower, which was under the direction of a lay staff member. It quickly became one of my favorite parish engagements. I soon noticed something remarkable. While many parish activities (especially those committee meetings) drained me of physical, emotional, and spiritual energy, the RCIA work did not. In fact, it left me energized, eager for the next team meeting and the next session with the candidates. Even the challenges of the process seemed welcome to me. One of the great thrills of that first year of priesthood was getting to preside at the Easter Vigil, at which I baptized some of the catechumens I had been walking with for months.

During my second year in the parish, the RCIA director proposed that we abandon our traditional baptismal font, with its tiny bowl of water used for pouring a trickle over the heads of infants and adults, and go for Baptism by immersion. After obtaining the pastor's approval, he procured a piece of farm equipment, a large round metal tank used for watering livestock. Around this he built a beautiful wooden frame, nicely stained and finished, with two small staircases for entry and exit. When the next Easter Vigil came, I was again presiding. After the homily, the whole community gathered around that baptismal pool. I'll never forget the thrill of kicking off my shoes and entering the water, with the words of Romans 6 echoing in our ears: "Are you unaware that we who were baptized into Christ Jesus were baptized into his death? We were indeed buried with him through baptism into death, so that, just as Christ was raised from the dead by the glory of the Father, we too might live in newness of life." After blessing the water, I looked up into the faces of the baptismal candidates and exclaimed, "Come to the water!" One by one they came, some with tears streaming down their faces, overjoyed by the moment. I knew them. Some were young, some were older. All had done some sinning and searching. All had experienced brokenness. But they had been brought to this moment by the Holy Spirit along a long and crooked path to Christian faith. I poured the water lavishly over each one's entire body, speaking the traditional Trinitarian formula, "I baptize you in the name of the Father, and of the Son, and of the Holy Spirit," with a big lump in my own throat. Never had I experienced so much joy in a liturgy as I did singing the many "Alleluias!" of that night. Our shared celebration lasted long into the night.

I remained involved in the RCIA during the rest of my time at Little Flower, and loved nearly every minute of it. Certainly, there were challenges at times. When people had to wait for an annulment, it caused all of us frustration and concern. Occasionally people dropped out of the process without explanation, leaving us only to pray for them. Frequently pastoral conversations with candidates led into deep regions of grief and woundedness, and I could not always bring the Lord's healing where it was desperately needed. But, time and again, I saw miracles of genuine healing, authentic conversion, new or expanded faith, and lives in which old patterns were set aside and new eagerness to serve was born. When it came time for me to move on, the most difficult thing for me to set aside was this work with catechumens and candidates for full communion with the Church. Those formative years have continued to guide me ever since.

What makes the initiation process so life giving for so many? In my experience at Little Flower, the RCIA left nearly everyone involved in it changed for the better in some way, and not only the candidates for Baptism and full communion with the Church. In varying ways and degrees, sponsors, spouses, catechists, and the wider parish community all found their faith renewed and deepened through accompanying the candidates and celebrating with them. My experience suggested the thesis for this book: *Done well, the rites and processes of Christian initiation can be one of the most powerful engines of disciple-making in the parish.*

How does that happen? There may be multiple answers, but let me mention two that I think are especially important.

Firstly, the *Rite of Christian Initiation of Adults* is unapologetically scriptural and Christocentric. It initiates new members into a community with a peculiar kind of faith, a people gathered by the Paschal Mystery. The life, death, and resurrection of Jesus Christ is visibly central in the readings we hear and in the central rituals we perform, thinking especially of Baptism and Eucharist. The RCIA, then, conducts initiands not into some vague kind of deism or diffuse new age spirituality, but into a specific, historical community gathered around the way marked out for us by Jesus of Nazareth. While we acknowledge many roads to God, and see God's grace at work well beyond the confines of our Church, the RCIA has a way of holding us to strict account around the central mysteries of our tradition's witness to God's self-revelation and action in history. It is clear about the essential nature of Christian identity, without being overly rigid or exclusive, and while being respectful of the individual's faith journey and unique giftedness.

Secondly, the RCIA has a holistic appeal, engendering a holistic conversion and holistic discipleship. This arises from the fact that it is composed of not only of words, but words of a particular kind joined to sacramental enactment and participation in service, what David Tracy called the way of "manifestation."[1] The process envisioned by the RCIA does demand serious study of the Scriptures and serious attention to the verbal communication essential to good catechesis. But it demands these be backed up with the special eloquence to be found in serious and

---

1. See David Tracy, *The Analogical Imagination* (New York: Crossroad, 1981).

reverent attention to liturgy and in the works of mercy in the wider human community. Little Flower was a parish where liturgy was already carefully prepared and celebrated joyfully. The music was top-notch and involved many people. There was a tradition of serious attention to the preaching, which made those of us who preached regularly even more diligent in constructing homilies. Moreover, the parish had a long history of being an active, service-oriented parish. Its relief efforts for the poor and its members' engagement in social justice efforts were already well known throughout our region. The flourishing of the RCIA at Little Flower Parish both built upon and further enhanced these strengths.

For me, the RCIA process proved to be extraordinarily integrating. I was challenged both to become a better listener and to become a better preacher and catechist, and to understand and embrace the necessary interplay among these roles. In the context of the RCIA, good pastoral care goes hand in hand with good preaching and good catechesis. I was immeasurably blessed and changed by the people I was privileged to walk with at such a deep and personal level. I was challenged to become the kind of spiritual leader my ordination called me to be, while at the same time becoming a good collaborator, one who recognizes, calls forth, and makes room for the gifts of many others in the community. In the context of the RCIA, one's leadership skills are on the line, yet the process has so many facets, so many people, so many moving parts, that it demands serious commitment to a team approach to ministry. At Little Flower, I was fortunate to work with a truly remarkable group of lay leaders on our RCIA team, and we remain friends to this day.

A key dynamic within the RCIA is that it proceeds incrementally, step-by-step toward the ultimate goal of full initiation. In other words, it is a journey, and its narrative both expresses and shapes the individual journeys of the participants. Excitement, interest, and expectation build as the process goes along. With each new stage and the ritual by which that stage is entered, the candidates and their companions sense that something is added, a new invitation is issued, and a deeper dimension is being laid bare for exploration. The nature of these stages and liturgical moments should be well understood by all of those called to preach, catechize, or accompany as sponsors. The RCIA itself presumes that those working within it have an intimate understanding of the scriptural texts, themes, ritual gestures, and elements of each season and rite. The pages that follow aim not only to build upon but also deepen the reader's grasp of the basic structure of the process. (See the *Outline for Christian Initiation for Adults* below.)

It is true, of course, that once the Easter Vigil has come and gone, it is difficult to sustain the same level of engagement that marked the journey up to the sacraments of initiation. We faced this at Little Flower, just as it is commonly reported elsewhere. Yet, in part, this experience challenges us to reappraise the ongoing life of our parishes. What kind of parish community is assumed by the RCIA? What kind of community is necessary both to host that process and to sustain the men and women who journey it beyond Easter? How might we reimagine parish life with the ongoing practice of Christian initiation at its vital center? We will begin here with some reflections on these very questions.

OUTLINE FOR CHRISTIAN INITIATION OF ADULTS

PERIOD OF EVANGELIZATION AND PRECATECHUMENATE

This is a time, of no fixed duration or structure, for inquiry and introduction to Gospel values, an opportunity for the beginnings of faith.

FIRST STEP: ACCEPTANCE INTO THE ORDER OF CATECHUMENS

This is the liturgical rite, usually celebrated on some annual date or dates, marking the beginning of the catechumenate proper, as the candidates express and the Church accepts their intention to respond to God's call to follow the way of Christ.

PERIOD OF THE CATECHUMENATE

This is the time, in duration corresponding to the progress of the individual, for the nurturing and growth of the catechumens' faith and conversion to God; celebrations of the word and prayers of exorcism and blessing are meant to assist the process.

SECOND STEP: ELECTION OR ENROLLMENT OF NAMES

This is the liturgical rite, usually celebrated on the First Sunday of Lent, by which the Church formally ratifies the catechumens' readiness for the sacraments of initiation and the catechumens, now the elect, express the will to receive these sacraments.

PERIOD OF PURIFICATION AND ENLIGHTENMENT

This is the time immediately preceding the elects' initiation, usually the Lenten season preceding the celebration of this initiation at the Easter Vigil; it is a time of reflection, intensely centered on conversion, marked by celebration of the scrutinies and presentations and of the preparation rites on Holy Saturday.

THIRD STEP: CELEBRATION OF THE SACRAMENTS OF INITIATION

This is the liturgical rite, usually integrated into the Easter Vigil, by which the elect are initiated through baptism, confirmation, and the eucharist.

PERIOD OF POSTBAPTISMAL CATECHESIS OR MYSTAGOGY

This is the time, usually the Easter season, following the celebration of initiation, during which the newly initiated experience being fully a part of the Christian community by means of pertinent catechesis and particularly by participation with all the faithful in the Sunday eucharistic celebration.

Abbreviations

EG	*Evangelii Gaudium: The Joy of the Gospel*
EN	*Evangelii Nuntiandi: Evangelization in the Modern World*
RCIA	*Rite of Christian Initiation of Adults*
RM	*The Roman Missal*
SC	*Sacrosanctum Concilium: Constitution on the Sacred Liturgy*
UR	*Unitatis Redintegratio: Decree on Ecumenism*

Chapter 1

The Parish Community as the Context of the Initiation Process

The parish is where the Church lives. Parishes are communities of faith, of action, and of hope. They are where the gospel is proclaimed and celebrated, where believers are formed and sent to renew the earth. Parishes are the home of the Christian community; they are the heart of our Church. Parishes are the place where God's people meet Jesus in word and sacrament and come in touch with the source of the Church's life.[1]

US Conference of Catholic Bishops

The Christian Initiation Process

The *Rite of Christian Initiation of Adults* sets out a comprehensive, holistic process for the incorporation of new members. Much more than a delivery system for a set of instructions and services, more than a set of formalized steps for full membership in an organization, the RCIA proposes to invite every aspect of the human person to conversion and discipleship. The scope is both breathtakingly exciting and sometimes daunting, as well.

When we speak of "Christian initiation," what are we initiating people *into*? The first and best answer, of course, is that we are initiating them *into Christ*. As the opening lines of the RCIA text say,

The rite of Christian initiation presented here is designed for adults who, after hearing the mystery of Christ proclaimed, consciously and freely seek the living God and enter the way of faith and conversion as the Holy Spirit opens their hearts. By God's help they will be strengthened spiritually during

---

1. United States Conference of Catholic Bishops, *Communities of Salt and Light: Reflections on the Social Mission of the Parish* (United States Catholic Conference, 1994), 1.

1

their preparation and at the proper time will receive the sacraments fruit-
fully. (RCIA, 1)

The initiative is Christ's, and the catechumen belongs to Christ. The
process is meant to cooperate with Christ's action, resulting in fruitful
reception of the sacraments.

The New Testament is very clear that the invitation is not only to
meet Christ as teacher, savior, and friend, but it is also in some sense
to step into the person of Christ, to be united with, joined to his person
in a mystical union that embraces and transforms our own personality.
St. Paul emphasizes that this immersion into Christ means all aspects of
Christ's story, going so far as to include his suffering and death: "Are you
unaware that we who were baptized into Christ Jesus are baptized into
his death?" (Romans 6:3). Both catechists and preachers connected to
initiation ministry must bear in mind that the goal of the initiation
process is always an encounter with the Living Christ. That encounter
gives membership in the Church more than a formalized meaning. That
encounter can heal, transform, and generate a life of generous, loving
service. Evoking an encounter with Christ is the goal of all catechesis
and preaching, not just when we have catechumens present.

Yet in the Catholic understanding of Christianity, initiation into
Christ is inseparable from initiation *into the Body of Christ, the Church*.
We are not offering a privatized discipleship to others. Following Christ
is always in company with others, and we are all both support and
challenge for one another. Christ calls and forms disciples as part of
a people. So we are initiating people into the Christian community,
the pilgrim People of God on earth.

Following the thinking of the New Testament further, then, our
understanding of being Church is always tensive (i.e., both universal
and local). One might say that Catholic ecclesiology has two poles.
The universal pole is represented by the universality of the Scriptures,
the liturgy, and the communion of bishops in union with the pope.
Together we make up the worldwide or "Catholic" Church that both
embraces and transcends particular cultures and contexts. The Rite of
Election, in which the bishop elects the catechumens sent to him from
throughout the diocese, is one instance in which those to be initiated
experience something of the marvelously broad and diverse communion

that makes up our Church. The bishop is, among other things, the focus of communion, the visible symbol of that unity in diversity.

At the other pole of our ecclesiology is the local worshiping community, the parish. A parish is not merely a franchisee of the universal Church; it *is* the Church, manifested and incarnated in a particular place and time and people, living in communion with other local communities the world over. It is where the sacraments are celebrated, where the Word is studied, preached, and shared and the locus from which the Christian mission to the world is launched. The parish's communion with other parishes in the diocese and throughout the world, through communion with the diocesan bishop, is an essential quality of parish life. Yet the parish community has an integrity, completeness, and indispensability of its own. It is where, on a week-to-week basis, God's people live, worship, and are nourished. As the US bishops have said, "The parish is where the Church lives."

What Kind of Parish Does the RCIA Call Us to Be?

The RCIA assumes that the process it outlines is going to be celebrated and enacted in the environment of a parish. While initiation is sometimes done in other contexts—for example, college campuses, prisons, military bases—there is no question that for the Rite the parish context is the normal home of both the liturgical celebrations marking the initiation journey and the catechetical process with which those celebrations are joined.

But there are all sorts of parishes on the worldwide Catholic landscape. What sort of parish does the Rite presume? To fully enact the Rite, what qualities, activities, and characteristics should we cultivate in our parishes? This is a crucially important yet often overlooked question. To answer it we will need to consult the text of the RCIA, as well as turn to the accumulated wisdom and experience of parishes where initiation ministry is thriving, to see what we can learn to complete our portrait of the parish as host of the initiation process. As we do this, a picture will emerge that is at once dynamic and exciting, challenging and idealistic.

As we turn to the text of the Rite, we may wish we could find an extended and explicit treatment of this theme, a concrete and complete description of the RCIA's parish home, but we do not. There are some foundational insights, but we will have to do some reading between the lines. Clearly the official authors understood that, while there are some essential aspects for any parish, the Rite would have to take root adaptively in varying local circumstances.[2] Hence, they were rightly wary of being too prescriptive.

In the introduction of the RCIA, initiation is described as "a gradual process that takes place within the community of the faithful [who] join the catechumens in reflecting on the value of the paschal mystery and by renewing their own conversion" (RCIA, 4). Indeed, "the entire community must help the candidates and the catechumens throughout the process of initiation" (RCIA, 9). Initiation is a "spiritual journey" (5) marked by certain "steps" (6) that have both private and public manifestations. A stable, concrete, welcoming community is being envisioned here, one committed to faithfully accompanying the candidates over a significant period of time. The introduction also previews some of the many ministers who have a role to play: the bishop, priests, deacons, catechists, sponsors, godparents. Without question, a lot of time and effort are being anticipated here. We can infer that initiation must be one of the most important and most complex things a Christian community ever does.

The assumptions about what it means to be an initiating parish come into somewhat sharper view in paragraph 75, which describes the Period of the Catechumenate. The subparagraphs reflect an ancient, fourfold understanding of the meaning of Church—four essential dimensions, we might say, of being Church.[3] The four dimensions take

---

2. See, for instance, RCIA, 2.

3. The precise origins of this patristic ecclesiology are not clear. Certainly, the framework rests in reflection upon Acts 2 and other New Testament texts. In some ancient sources: *didache* (training, teaching) and/or *martyria* (witness) are included in the scheme or substituted for *kerygma* or *diakonia*. James B. Dunning discusses the fourfold understanding utilized here in his *Echoing God's Word: Formation for Catechists and Homilists in a Catechumenal Church* (Chicago: Liturgy Training Publications, 1993), 100–138. As Dunning says: "Our ministry to catechumens and their ministry to us is grounded in the real presence of Christ in the community, which is the Body of Christ. That community lives and shares Christ's presence by proclaiming his message, developing community, offering worship to God and service to God's people–the dimensions and dynamics of catechesis found in paragraph 75" (102f.).

place simultaneously and interlock with one another. Let's examine each of them in turn.

Kerygma: The Word Proclaimed

A suitable catechesis is provided by priests or deacons, or by catechists and others of the faithful, planned to be gradual and complete in its coverage, accommodated to the liturgical year, and solidly supported by celebrations of the word. This catechesis leads the catechumens not only to an appropriate acquaintance with dogmas and precepts but also to a profound sense of the mystery of salvation in which they desire to participate. (RCIA, 75.1)

The catechumens are, first of all, learners. The local church provides them with formation that impresses the importance of Christian truth not only upon their minds but upon their hearts and wills, as well. Celebrations of the Word are at the center of this learning program. The Church's doctrinal and dogmatic traditions guide the presentation of the faith, and a certain degree of basic familiarity with those traditions is desirable for the candidates. Those who lead this program must bear in mind that doctrine is not in competition with Scripture, not to be set over against Scripture, but is indeed thoroughly scriptural in its very nature. Doctrine functions both to save from error and to invite into a world of interpretation—or, we might just as easily say, a world in which we are interpreted. As the Word is proclaimed, our rich doctrinal tradition invites the hearers to listen and immerse themselves in it, finding in it the life-giving treasures that generations of hearers before us have discovered.

Moreover, the paragraph reminds us that the goal is more than cognitive knowledge of the necessarily formulaic language of doctrine and catechisms. That would be the sort of knowledge that our common experiences of "school" usually denote, but the Rite is directing us to something even more than that. The deeper goal is for the candidates to participate in the mysteries expressed. Christian truth is by nature participatory, and it embraces and integrates the whole person. The participation aimed at here is not only public and liturgical but also interior and prayerful, resulting in a transformed life.

The sacred mysteries into which we invite the catechumens to plunge are not completely beyond comprehension nor experience. The biblical sense of mystery is better expressed as "that which is infinitely intelligible." Judeo-Christian belief stresses that nothing less than God's self-revelation is on offer. Yet God's infinitude means that none of us will ever fully grasp it, at least not in this life.

The text of the Rite indicates that the desired catechesis should be "complete in its coverage," and "presenting Catholic teaching in its entirety" (RCIA, 78). The meaning of these phrases is not immediately clear. Do they mean that the catechumen knows the whole Bible? The whole of the *Catechism of the Catholic Church*? But such a goal could only be approached asymptotically through many years of study! James Dunning emphasizes that the "completeness" sought here should be thought of qualitatively, not quantitatively.[4] It is probably best understood through its close association with the phrase that follows, which bids us to follow the course of the liturgical year. Arguably, in a single liturgical year all of the major truths of Christian faith are encountered and celebrated. As the Fathers of the Second Vatican Council said:

> In the course of the [liturgical] year . . . [the church] unfolds the whole mystery of Christ from the incarnation and nativity to the ascension, to Pentecost and the expectation of the blessed hope of the coming of the Lord.[5]

The liturgical cycle, then, has a kind of essential wholeness or completeness to it. This interpretation would seem to be supported by the Rite's suggestion in RCIA, 76, that the period of the catechumenate could be "several years if necessary." One entire liturgical year is likely the implied minimum to achieve a kind of initial complete foundation on which to build a lifetime of growth.

Dunning also says that completeness of catechesis must also consider the Second Vatican Council's advance of the idea that there is a "hierarchy of truths"[6] in the Christian faith.[7] Although the Council did not spell this hierarchy out, presumably it means that there is an ordered relationship among Christian doctrines, in which some truths are foundational for others. For example, patristic scholar John Cavadini says,

---

4. Dunning, *Echoing God's Word*, 110.

5. *Sacrosanctum Concilium*, 102; revised Flannery translation.

6. *Unitatis Redintegratio: The Decree on Ecumenism*, 11.

7. Dunning, *Echoing God's Word*, 110. The author also cites the 1971 *General Catechetical Directory*, which states, "On all levels, catechesis should take account of this hierarchy of the truths of the faith" (43).

Aren't all the basic doctrines of the Church, those high up in the "hierarchy of truths," doctrines of the divine Love? The doctrine of creation, of the Trinity, of the Incarnation, of the Holy Spirit, the Church and the communion of saints: these are all in some way attempts to express and specify the central mysteries of God's love.[8]

The truths affirmed in the baptismal formula—to be used in the celebration of the catechumens' Baptism sometime hence—would be the most foundational and thus most immediately relevant to catechumenal catechesis. Perhaps a second tier of truths to be explored is expressed in the Creed, and around that Collect various other doctrinal affirmations not found in the text of the Creed itself.

The parish community that can provide and sustain the sort of comprehensive catechesis proposed in this paragraph will be one in which, in multiple ways, it is plain that the Word of God is preeminent and actively sought out for the light it sheds on our lives. What will this parish look like? This will be apparent, firstly, through the quality of preaching and liturgical celebration. Liturgical preaching can go a long way toward communicating and inviting the hearer into an active role for the Scriptures in a person's daily life. Preaching's power is enhanced by liturgies that are carefully prepared, with high quality and inviting music, an active ministry of hospitality, and other factors. Additional, non-Eucharistic preaching occasions, including some in which qualified lay preachers give witness, can complement and reinforce the Sunday message. Nevertheless, an active, alive praxis of *kerygma* will be demonstrated in other ways too: the quality of catechesis provided to children, Bible studies and other adult faith formation programs, the love and adherence to the Word demonstrated in parish committee meetings, the use of various technological media for evangelization, and so on. The vision here is of a parish community permeated with the proclamation of the Good News, a proclamation with a vigorous outreach to others. We will examine the practice of evangelization further below.

---

8. John C. Cavadini, "On Teaching Christianity," *Church Life Journal* (August 1, 2016), https://churchlife.nd.edu/2016/08/01/on-teaching-christianity/.

Koinonia: Community or Fellowship

RCIA 75.2, the longest of the four subparagraphs, reads in part:

> As they become familiar with the Christian way of life and are helped by
> the example and support of sponsors, godparents, and the entire Christian
> community, the catechumens learn to turn more readily to God in prayer,
> to bear witness to the faith, in all things to keep their hopes set on Christ,
> to follow supernatural inspiration in their deeds, and to practice love of
> neighbor, even at the cost of self-renunciation.

This text suggests that a concrete Christian community is something
more than a passive context for the initiation journey. The assumption
here is that the community plays an active role by both example and
support, helping the catechumens learn to pray, learn to bear their own
personal witness to Christ, and learn to shape their conduct in generous,
compassionate, loving ways. Catechumens notice the example of
community members who visit the sick, take food baskets to shut-ins
and the poor, or volunteer to help with the youth group. They are being
introduced into a whole way of life, and certain aspects of that life are
better "caught" than "taught." It is through others that love moves from
the merely conceptual to the concrete. We learn what self-emptying love
is from parents, friends, teachers, mentors, as we observe how they live,
the quality of their relationships, and the sacrifices they make. We also
learn that such love can be personally costly, but that at such times we
are not alone—we have the support of fellow travelers. Others in the
Christian community literally lead us to God. Christian faith has a social
dimension. As Vatican II taught us, the assembled community is one of
the four ways in which we meet Christ at the liturgy (SC, 7).

Much of this communal accompaniment and mentorship
occurs informally. The presence of others at community liturgies and
celebrations provides strength in numbers and witness to a life of faith.
Conversations are struck up after Mass, over coffee and donuts and
potluck suppers, and among neighbors. Here community issues are
discussed, personal support is offered, struggles are shared. But it takes
deliberate form through catechists, sponsors, godparents, spiritual
directors, and often, spouses. The leaders of a community plan
intentionally for the needs of the catechumens so that they share in a
lively experience of community. But community leaders plan ways to

nurture such communal bonds for all members of the parish, as well. Not infrequently it is that experience of meaningful community—whether through the vibrancy of the liturgy, the parish's social outreach, the after-Mass celebrations, or some combination of these—which drew the catechumens to the parish in the first place.

Sadly, too many of our parishes today continue to be experienced by many people as dry, impersonal places offering too little human warmth and interaction. Too many Catholics continue to approach the Sunday Eucharist in a silent, passive, almost privatized devotional kind of way. At the same time, many parishes have worked hard and successfully to generate an atmosphere of hospitality, camaraderie, and mutual support. You can sense the difference almost as soon as you cross the threshold of the church sanctuary. Parishes with a vigorous initiation process often also have a panoply of community options for all their members: small Christian communities, support groups, an active parish pastoral council, committees and task groups, parish-wide celebrations of special feasts, and so on. Active engagement in these sorts of parish subgroupings helps to form ordinary parishioners in the value of community, predisposing them to play an active role in welcoming and supporting inquirers, catechumens, the elect, and the newly initiated.

Of course, Christian community is not an end in itself, a fact that sets the Church apart from some other human communities. It must remain centered on its Lord and its Lord's mission, in which it shares. The alert preacher will find many opportunities in the yearly Lectionary to preach about the nature of being Church for one another. The innately communal character of both the Old and the New Testaments is not always readily apparent nor easily understood in our individualistic culture. Good preaching is vital both to nurturing *koinonia* and to keeping it on mission. Healthy communion with others is indeed part of God's good news for us. Brotherhood/sisterhood with other believers is more than a nice notion; it needs to be, and can be, experienced and cultivated as an important dimension of daily life. Indeed, community is one of the Lord's instruments for bringing about in all of us "a progressive change of outlook and conduct" (RCIA, 75.2), which is the slow, endless work of grace in us producing conversion.

Leitourgia: Worship and Prayer

The third subparagraph of RCIA 75 begins:

> The Church, like a mother, helps the catechumens on their journey by means of suitable liturgical rites, which purify the catechumens little by little and strengthen them with God's blessing. Celebrations of the Word of God are arranged for their benefit, and at Mass they may also take part with the faithful in the liturgy of the word, thus better preparing themselves for their eventual participation in the liturgy of the Eucharist.

In our secularized, technologically driven, rationalistic culture there is an invidious tendency to dismiss ritual as a kind of formalized activity that is optional, even superficial, and perhaps extraneous to the matters of real substance with which life is concerned. This reductionistic tendency can sometimes even infect the Church, as well, and it is not unknown in initiation ministry. Catechetical leaders can subtly convey the notion that catechesis is the "real stuff" of the process, while liturgical celebrations merely enhance or provide ornamentation to that. Some initiation ministries fall prey to a differentiation of labor in which the liturgical aspect is "left to Father," thus seeming to divorce it from the other aspects of the process.

For Catholic Christians, liturgical worship is never merely ornamental. Indeed, it is the center and lifeblood of the community precisely as Church. Worship of the Triune God is the Christian community's first priority. Likewise, the RCIA affirms that liturgical celebrations are vitally important for those on the path of initiation. Liturgy has real power, power to "purify" and "strengthen" those who participate in it, and its grace plays a role in the ongoing transformation of the catechumens, no less than the fully initiated.

Moreover, the subparagraph envisions the catechumens taking part in a wide variety of liturgical celebrations. It assumes that the catechumens will be attending the Sunday Eucharist regularly. The liturgy, and especially the homily, constitutes a central part of the catechumens' catechesis. As Robert Duggan and Maureen Kelly have pointed out, "ritual experience itself is catechetical and formative, at a level and with a power that no formal instruction can emulate."[9] Even

---

9. Robert Duggan and Maureen Kelly, *The Christian Initiation of Children: Hope for the Future* (Paulist Press, 1991), 34.

though they are not full participants, and ordinarily should be dismissed from the liturgical assembly before the Liturgy of the Eucharist begins, they are nonetheless regarded as members of the household of faith who join in the praise of God as they are able. The centrality of the Sunday liturgy is often powerfully experienced by catechumens in the way the Word of God is unfolded, first in the proclamation of the Scripture readings, then in the homily, and later in the catechetical or "breaking open the Word" session that follows the dismissal. The soundest approach to catechumenal catechesis is to coordinate it closely with the Sunday Scripture readings, allowing the Lectionary to prompt and direct the catechetical agenda for a given week.

However, the liturgical experience of the catechumens is not limited to the Sunday eucharistic assembly. The Rite envisions other liturgical celebrations, some of them public, amid the full liturgical assembly (e.g., the Rite of Becoming Catechumens, the Rite of Sending, the Scrutinies) and some of them held just with the group of catechumens and their catechists and sponsors. Some creativity is invited here; special celebrations of the Word of the Lord designed for the catechumens should punctuate the process frequently. In addition, catechumens can be invited and encouraged to attend parish celebrations of the Liturgy of the Hours, the non-sacramental part of Reconciliation services, special prayer vigils and devotions, healing prayer services, and the like.

The initiating parish will strive to be a place where the liturgical life is rich and full. This means something far more than merely scheduling masses at convenient times. It means doing the liturgy well, with all the attention and care for detail that it deserves. Good liturgy allows the symbols, images, gestures, and spoken texts to speak with the all the robust power they in fact contain. A well-done Sunday liturgy requires an amazing collaboration of well-formed ministers of different kinds: hospitality, music, lectors, deacon, priest, and others. In a parish in the habit of doing liturgy well, the assembly readily plays its part, too, in "full, active and conscious participation." Good liturgy has a leisurely yet dynamic and intentional flow to it. As Dunning says beautifully:

> A community alive to worship and witness, which goes out to welcome candidates; signs them with the cross from head to foot; proclaims the word with fidelity; testifies at election to what God has been doing in their lives;

lays on hands in solidarity in the Spirit for healing; immerses in water that recalls the waters over which God's Spirit bent low at creation and flood and exodus; generously anoints them with the oil of priests, prophets, kings and martyr-witnesses; and shares their brokenness in broken bread and shared wine—all these strong and authentic images can invite catechumens into worship, into exodus, into death and resurrection.[10]

Good liturgy is moving, powerful, transformative. These same qualities will mark the array of special occasion or non-eucharistic liturgical occasions, which characterize the parish too: funerals, weddings, infant Baptisms, the Liturgy of the Hours, Reconciliation, Anointing, and so on. Initiation ministry thrives where a parish is constantly moving from celebration to celebration.

Preaching plays an important role in the liturgical life of the parish. One of the distinctive things about the Catholic understanding of liturgical preaching is that the homily is seen not as an interruption in the liturgy but as part of it. The homily is thus a form of the worship of God. The homily is never to be omitted at Sunday Mass, and ordinarily should be included in daily Masses and other sacramental celebrations as well. While preaching may or may not be included in other celebrations (e.g., Reconciliation services, the Liturgy of the Hours), including some brief preaching may be a good opportunity for the spiritual edification of the participants. Such occasions can also be opportunities for well-prepared preaching by qualified non-ordained people. It is vitally important that catechumens—and all of us—hear the witness of faith from a variety of people in all walks of life. Lay preaching complements, and does not compete with, the preaching of the ordained.

The need for well-prepared, effective preaching hardly needs to be stressed here. Priests and deacons must make the time needed to discern and construct the homily a priority every week, and this is not easy amid the many claims on their time. Multiple studies have shown that the two most important factors in the congregation's experience of the liturgy are the quality of the music and the quality of the preaching. Both require resources of time and treasure.

Preachers in initiating parishes will want to give special attention to a mystagogical approach to preaching, in which the meaning of the

---

10. Dunning, *Echoing God's Word*, 121.

liturgical actions, gestures, materials, and words is savored and unfolded for the hearers. Our tradition, and especially the heritage of the patristic period, contains a wealth of mystagogical preaching. Contemporary Catholic preaching could benefit from a re-appropriation of a kind of reflective spiritual pondering of the Church's rites. Moreover, mystagogical preaching is not just appropriate during the Period of Mystagogy for the newly baptized, but can be used in a major or minor key any time during the church year. The whole character of the Christian life is mystagogical. We are a baptismal people, always coming from and returning to the Table.

Diakonia: Service in Mission

> Since the Church's life is apostolic, catechumens should also learn how to work actively with others to spread the Gospel and build up the Church by the witness of their lives and by professing their faith. (RCIA, 75.4)

This is by far the shortest of the four subparagraphs of paragraph RCIA, 75. Perhaps its brevity contributes to its being the most commonly overlooked aspect of the catechumenate. As the text says, the Church is by nature apostolic, active, and outward looking. The catechumens are being inducted into a faith community with a mission to serve not only other members of the Church but the wider world. That service is part and parcel of the witness of the faith, which is to say, it is intimately united with our mission to evangelize the world. The Eucharist itself is intimately linked with the call to wash the feet of the world.

Catholic institutions, including parishes, provide an amazing array of social services geared especially for those who are poor or in special need. At the same time, Catholics tend to be shy about explicit evangelization (i.e., about speaking personally of the quality of their faith and hope in Christ) and inviting others to consider investigating their parish. Parishes that actively evangelize in these explicit ways are rare indeed. Most parishes do have within their structure some outreach efforts to youth and charitable relief efforts for the local poor, such as a food pantry, St. Vincent de Paul Society, or a soup kitchen. Parish groupings from the Knights of Columbus to the youth group to the Social Action Committee pitch in to assist with local needs and civic betterment projects. Too often, the reigning assumption is that social ministry and evangelization belong to separate spheres and have nothing to do with one another. Yet the Church, from Vatican II's *Gaudium et Spes* and *Ad Gentes* through Paul VI's *Populorum Progressio* and *Evangelii Nuntiandi*, through John Paul II, Benedict XVI, and Francis, has repeatedly insisted that these spring from a single well of motivation, namely, the mission of Jesus Christ himself.

In my experience, not many initiation ministries seem to do well with introducing new members into their roles as witness-servants. We could do better, for example, at acknowledging and embracing the fact that already as catechumens these men and women are ministering to us: through their very desire to join us and grow in faith, through their eagerness to break open the Word, through symbolical witness to us in dismissal from the Sunday Eucharist and the roles they plan standing before us at the other rites. Frequently the explicit *diakonia* aspect of the catechesis offered to them is reduced to a superficial introduction to the various ministries of the community (e.g., catechesis of the young, liturgical ministries of lector and extraordinary ministers of Holy Communion, parish council and committees). While these "churchy" ministries are important, exclusive focus on them can neglect the repeated biblical thrust to go to the wider world with a message of hope and good news, preached and enacted. The Second Vatican Council emphasized that it is in the world, not in the Church as such, that most baptized Christians live out their baptismal call to mission.[11] Indeed, the full restoration of this baptismal emphasis remains the largest unmet challenge of the Council more than fifty years later.

Perhaps it is thought that the catechetical needs of the catechumens are so pressing as to preclude time to introduce them to forms of outward mission, as if, again, the real business of the catechumenate is purely catechetical and the outflow into service will be acquired after the Easter. This is a serious mistake. We need to be reminded of the Rite's insistence that the catechumens are being introduced to a whole way of life, not just a package of truths, but "a progressive change of outlook and conduct . . . [with] social consequences" (RCIA,75.2). Another factor leading to the truncation of *diakonia* in the catechumenate is the all too

---

11. See especially *Apostolicam Actuositatem* and *Gaudium et Spes*.

common compression of the process into the confines of the school year. Instead of a full year or more, the catechumenate is reduced to a weekly hour or two in the seven months from September to Easter. This brief timetable carries with it a lot of pressure to "get everything in," and the service aspect is neglected. When mission is neglected, we are also withholding from the catechumens not only a responsibility that is rightly theirs, but withholding too a means by which Christians meet the Living Christ. "Whatever you did to the least of these, you did for me" (Matthew 25:40). Paragraph 75.4 might have served us well to remind us that it is in mission, in serving others, that we also meet the face of Christ himself. We owe it to catechumens to afford them opportunities to join in service projects, outreach efforts, feeding the hungry, peace and justice ministries, and the various ways by which Christians seek to live and give witness to their faith in their jobs, families, and civil communities.

Liturgical preachers in our parishes can assist here too. The Lectionary texts offer us multiple opportunities for reflecting on our gracious call to be part of what the Lord is doing among his people. Preachers can help to dispel the fear that often surrounds evangelization by illustrating concrete ways to do this responsibly and respectfully, in tandem with other forms of service. They can point out the needs both within and surrounding a parish community and suggest ways to address those needs. Examples include the divorced and separated who often populate the rear pews in our churches; young people who have distinct needs in a community without a youth ministry program; the hungry and homeless who roam the neighborhood streets or remain in quiet desperation behind the doors in local apartment complexes. Preaching calls us to be our best, most generous selves. Far from a burden or a mere moral imperative, *diakonia* is a joy and an enrichment of our spirituality, a life of freedom from excessive self-preoccupation. Not only that, the weekly Eucharist itself reminds us that as we are nourished, strengthened, and healed, so we are to assist in nourishing, strengthening, and healing the world. Preachers above all should want their hearers to encounter the Lord in the multiple ways he comes to us: in communal worship and sacrament, in private prayer, in others, in mission. Christ—

who came as servant, taking the lowest place, "emptying himself" (Philippians 2:7)—is our model and inspiration.

While each is distinct, there is a circularity and interpenetration of these four dimensions of Church with one another. The Word of life generates community, permeates the liturgy, and spurs to action. Lived community thrives on the proclamation of the Word, gathers around the sacraments, and is sent on mission. The liturgy is a creature of the Word, forms and celebrates the Body of Christ, and nourishes mission. Service sheds new light on the Word passed down to us, nurtures a special kind of fraternity/sorority, and leads us to present all human need for offering on the Table. Each dimension requires the others. Well integrated, they are no more than four facets of one way of life lived communally yet uniquely by each believer.

To conclude this brief snapshot of the parish host of initiation ministry, let us turn to some further reflections on leadership, evangelization, and the role of preaching.

Chapter 2

Becoming an Initiating Parish: A Leadership Guide

Christian leaders who embrace and value collaborative approaches to ministry discover the power of involving others. The sum is so much greater than the parts. Collaborative leaders do not act in isolation. They are inclusive rather than exclusive in approach. They are willing to listen to and collaborate with those whose views and style may differ from their own. Being collaborative taps into the gifts of many people, fosters creativity, and achieves greater results.[1]

Loughlan Sofield, ST, and Donald H. Kuhn

As we have seen, the RCIA presumes that a number of different people will be assisting in the process: clergy, catechists, sponsors, and the like. While it is possible, indeed not that uncommon, to conceive and perform these roles as specialized forms of service in a degree of isolation from one another, they are better to be regarded as a team.

Who's in Charge? A Primer in Team Dynamics

In team ministry, I have found that roles overlap and interlock with one another, and there is a deliberate kind of working in coordination with one another. While team members have tasks for which they are individually responsible or co-responsible, the team is jointly responsible for the major goals of the process. Some tasks, and some special needs that arise in the course of the process, often require the assistance of more than one team member or even all of them. Team members assist one another and consult one another regularly. While the expertise of each

---

1. Loughlan Sofield, ST, and Donald H. Kuhn, *The Collaborative Leader: Listening to the Wisdom of God's People* (Notre Dame, IN: Ave Maria Press, 1995), 38.

is respected and elicited, no one works in complete isolation from the others. Team ministry requires a strong commitment to communication and listening to other team members and to the catechumens, and a willingness to yield to the wishes and needs of others discovered through healthy group process.

Sometimes this model of leadership is termed *shared leadership*. The phrase is not without appeal. On the face of it, it sounds egalitarian and connotes a generosity of spirit and a non-defensive, non-dominating, unselfish engagement in ministry, which the Gospel surely encourages. "Sharing" sounds like something virtuous, a practice Christians would want to be part of, and even become good at. In actual practice, however, I find that too often *shared leadership* signals two unfortunate and closely related things. One is that, put simply, *leadership* is sometimes diluted at the expense of *sharing*. As some wag has said, "if everyone is in charge, no one is in charge." The process needs real *leadership*, and that means a robust exercise of authority in various ways. A team that gets bogged down in its own internal process may get too little accomplished, or may even become too inward-focused at the expense of its mission. Oversensitivity to not stepping on others' toes can even lead to missing the bigger picture of the whole initiation enterprise.

Second and more importantly, behind the phrase *shared leadership* sometimes lies a zero-sum assumption about leadership; that is to say, an assumption that there is only so much power to go around, and thus the holder of power—in this case, the parish pastor—has to divest himself of some power and divvy it up with others. The zero-sum assumption about power and authority must be opened up. The fact is that in every parish there already exist various kinds of leadership. Official leadership, the leadership that inheres in office, is vested in the pastor and other ordained ministers. Pastoral leadership is conferred, and remains accountable to the bishop, for the good of the faithful and the fidelity of the whole community to the mission of Christ and the Church. Pastors ought not, cannot trade away authority that is truly and legitimately theirs and theirs alone.

Other Leadership Gifts

But there are also various other kinds of gifts given by the Holy Spirit for leadership. For instance, as anyone who has worked in a parish knows, every parish has its saints: people who lead by the example of their personal holiness, prayerfulness, virtue, selflessness. Every parish has its Anna and Simeon figures, older folks who are always there, their faces set toward the sanctuary. Every parish has its unselfish, generous, competent organizers of charitable works, catechesis, building projects, and social occasions. Every parish has people with skills for fund-raising, stewardship of resources, and administration. With the right kind of leadership from the pastor, even more of these gifts for various kinds of leadership can be recognized, called forth, trained, supported, and woven into the fabric of community life.

For these and other reasons, I prefer to think of the leadership necessary to a flourishing initiation ministry—thinking here especially of the parish pastor, and also the leader of the initiation ministry team—as *collaborative leadership*.[2] This phrase better respects that everyone on a team has a unique and important leadership role to play, but they must work together for the common good of the parish community. There is a degree of specialization, and with that, a unique kind of authority borne by each member; yet each one needs and must actively cooperate with all the others. This fits St. Paul's metaphor of the Church as the Body of Christ, composed of many distinct members with unique roles to play, all coordinated for the body to get in motion. Active, deliberate collaboration in ministry entails skills that can be learned and improved in both initial and ongoing formation of the minister. The collaborative leader routinely assumes that he or she is part of a team in which the efforts of each complement and enhance the efforts of all others.

To the adjective *collaborative* I'm tempted to add another, *empowering*, which comes to mind and is commonly in use in the management world. What that word attempts to get at is a style of leadership that proactively discerns, calls forth, and supports the full range of leadership gifts the Spirit endows, coupled with a commitment to ensure that all collaborators have the kinds of authority, support, and resources they need to execute

---

2. See, *inter alia*, Sofield and Kuhn, *The Collaborative Leader*; and Loughlan Sofield, ST, and Carroll Juliano, SHCJ, *Collaboration: Uniting Our Gifts in Ministry* (Notre Dame, IN: Ave Maria Press, 2000).

their roles competently. Of course the problem with *empowering* is the implication that the power is conferred condescendingly; in this case, held by the pastor and bestowed on the laity. But the real source of empowerment is always the gift of the Spirit in Baptism, not the priest. So we need a different word, perhaps something like *evocative*, as the etymology of that word points to the "calling forth" aspect of good leadership. The point here is simply that the kind of leadership at the heart of a parish initiation team, and at the heart of the initiating parish, actively joins in concerted efforts with others, and actively, attentively seeks to discover the gifts of others, allowing the Spirit to generate more forms of service, more diversity of leadership, and a richer life for the whole parish community. The responsibilities that go with sacred office are important for the welfare of the community and must be respected, of course. However, official leadership is only one of many forms of leadership with which the Spirit endows a community. The working assumption in such a parish will be a diversified picture of different kinds of leadership and giftedness in concert with one another; a system that is at once dynamic, flexible, and growing. Such collaborative leadership teams can be messy, to be sure, and they will stretch the pastor's organizational ability, recruitment skills, and even patience. But the possible rewards are great: a greater reach for the parish's ministry, and participants who feel respected and invited to deeper discipleship themselves.

The collaborative, evocative pastor is not threatened by the gifts of others but rejoices in them, and places himself willingly at their service, knowing that in so doing he is cooperating with Christ himself. He considers himself the central, coordinating focal point of a beehive of activity—no small thing—but not the source of that activity. He has no need to try and do it all himself, for he knows gratefully that he cannot and need not. He wields the authority that is uniquely his gracefully, not as a burden but as an expression of service. He is a figure who leads not only by dint of office but by an obvious personal humility and deference to Christ. He is guided appropriately by the principle of subsidiarity, yet not afraid to exercise authority when it is clearly for the good of the community. He is at home in the weekly processes of collaboration with the whole range of parish ministries, and he actively prowls the community, looking for gifts of leadership and service that have not yet been recognized and tapped. He is a courageous, visionary leader in the sense that he relies upon the Spirit to help him see needs to be addressed, gifts to be affirmed and called forth, a more abundant life for the community and each of its members.

The Evangelizing Parish

Wherever the initiation process is being implemented in a conscientious way, it raises the question, "What are we of Saint X Parish doing to welcome others into our life?" The RCIA is the most powerful driver for a renewal of evangelization that the Catholic Church has seen in a long while. Not only does the text formally assert that initiation of new members is among our most important tasks as Church, it places responsibility for that task broadly on *all the baptized*. It also gathers momentum as it develops in a parish. As parishioners begin to see candidates and catechumens standing before them at the Sunday liturgies, finding something in the Christian life that they want to join, inevitably the fully initiated faithful are personally touched and moved, too, and in small or large ways they begin to take more seriously the Christian life and their own baptismal call to give witness and invitation to others.

Still, even today thirty years into the implementation of the Rite, there are relatively few of our parishes that can truly be described as actively and intentionally evangelizing communities. The promotion of a parish culture of evangelization faces some strong headwinds in a culture that is highly secularized and individualistic. Moreover, generations of Catholics, many of them deeply faithful, have been nurtured in a style of spirituality that has stressed ethical living but a fundamental privacy about essential matters of one's personal faith, rendering them passive in the public forum. They may care deeply about Christ, the Blessed Mother, the Catholic Church, and their own parish affiliation. That care may be amply demonstrated in their love of their families, their generosity in contributing time, talent, and treasure to the parish, and the quality of their citizenship in the wider society. But they find it exceedingly difficult to know how to speak of these things, to articulate what they mean, and how and why they may be of interest for others to consider. Contrast this with the religious style of some evangelical Protestants, who are so prominent on the American religious landscape. For them personal witness and outreach are high priorities. Whatever may be the limitations of their theology and approach, they do have a language for this mission ready at hand. In contrast, Catholics often appear meek and mute about their faith, even when they have personally discovered its treasures.

Under the influence of the RCIA and other developments, and given the considerable and increasingly obvious attrition of Catholics to secularization or to the evangelical and pentecostal churches, the situation seems to be slowly changing. Recent popes have urged Catholics to a renewed understanding and reinvigorated practice of evangelization. In fact, beginning with Vatican II's *Ad Gentes*, continuing through Paul VI's *Evangelii Nuntiandi*, through the repeated calls to "new evangelization" in the writings of John Paul II and Benedict XVI, and most recently in Francis' *Evangelii Gaudium*, the Catholic understanding of evangelization has undergone an exciting period of theological recovery and development. These developments are now reaching Catholic parishes and ministries through such programs as Cursillo and its several offshoots, RENEW International,[3] Christ Renews His Parish,[4] the Fellowship of Catholic University Students (FOCUS),[5] the *Rebuilt* series of Fr. Michael White and Tom Corcoran,[6] Fr. James Mallon's *Divine Renovation*,[7] and others. A succession of popes and a number of dioceses have named evangelization as one of their current pastoral priorities. Sherry Weddell's recent book, *Forming Intentional Disciples*,[8] seems to be generating some energetic discussion and pastoral planning.

---

3. See http://www.renewintl.org/.

4. See http://www.mycrhp.org/MYCRHP/Welcome.html.

5. See https://www.focus.org/.

6. See Michael White and Tom Corcoran, *Rebuilt: Awakening the Faithful, Reaching the Lost, and Making Church Matter* (Notre Dame, IN: Ave Maria Press, 2013). Also by these authors: *Tools for Rebuilding: 75 Really, Really Practical Ways to Make Your Parish Better* (Notre Dame, IN: Ave Maria Press, 2013); *Rebuilding Your Message: Practical Tools to Strengthen Your Preaching and Teaching* (Notre Dame, IN: Ave Maria Press, 2015); and *The Rebuilt Field Guide: Ten Steps for Getting Started* (Notre Dame, IN: Ave Maria Press, 2016).

7. James Mallon, *Divine Renovation: Bringing Your Parish from Maintenance to Mission* (New London, CT: Twenty-Third Publications, 2014).

8. Sherry Weddell, *Forming Intentional Disciples: The Path to Knowing and Following Jesus* (Huntington, IN: Our Sunday Visitor, 2012).

The parish that is a fit home for the RCIA will be a parish that sets evangelization as one of its highest priorities. Such a parish will set aside generous resources for its outreach efforts and devote clergy and staff time and talent to them as well. At the same time, such a parish will resist making evangelization the province of religious professionals alone. Competent leadership of evangelization is necessary, but the evangelizing parish will seek to motivate and equip all of its members to play their roles in the apostolic mission of their local church. Such a parish will also strive to avoid making evangelization just a specialized set of activities and programs, but seek to integrate the concern for outreach into all of its activities and structures.

The Role of Preaching

At the heart of the evangelizing parish, in which a vigorous initiation ministry takes root, one is almost certain to find a pastor who is a good, effective preacher. Truly outstanding preachers are as few in contemporary Catholicism as they have been in any age or in any church denomination. The charism for preaching is not given to all, but its discernment is undoubtedly one of the touchstones of the call to priestly and diaconal ministry. As the Second Vatican Council said, "the first task of priests . . . [is] to preach the Gospel of God to all."[9] Yet, while the John Chrysostoms, Fulton Sheens, and Walter Burghardts are rare in any age, consistent effectiveness in preaching is a bar to which every pastor and every associate pastor and deacon can and should aspire.

So what is effectiveness in preaching? The question deserves a longer answer than is possible here,[10] but a few basic points can be mentioned.

1. *Effective Catholic preaching leads the hearers to an encounter with a living God.* The first and most important goal of preaching is to bring people to God. As Pope Benedict XVI put it, "Being Christian is not the

---

9. *Presbyterorum Ordinis*, 4. Flannery revised translation.

10. For a more extensive treatment of effectiveness in Catholic preaching see the following four-part series by the author in the online *Church Life Journal* (Institute for Church Life, University of Notre Dame), September 2016 through January 2017:

http://churchlife.nd.edu/2016/09/28/effectivecatholicpreachingpart1/
http://churchlife.nd.edu/2016/10/12/effectivecatholicpreachingpart2/
http://churchlife.nd.edu/2016/11/09/effectivecatholicpreachingpart3/
http://churchlife.nd.edu/2017/01/25/effectivecatholicpreachingpart4/

result of an ethical choice or a lofty idea, but the encounter with an event, a person, which gives life a new horizon and a decisive direction."[11] Thus, it is not entertainment, eloquence, erudition, nor good humor that people need from preaching, but a way to find God. There are teaching moments within preaching, but they are within a larger aim to forge a love relationship between the hearer and God. Effective preaching is unitary—it has one and only one central message, a single thread of discovery and insight. It leaves the listener with a sense that God is near, reaching out a hand of friendship to the hearer. Shallow preaching doesn't cut it; people want substance, something that matters to their lives. Effective preaching is appropriately "spiritual," which does not mean ethereal nor remote but a word from God addressed to the deepest core of human longing. Liturgical preaching leads to worship and thanksgiving at the eucharistic table, and inspires private prayer and personal commitment. We long to hear people say to us, "Your preaching today brought me closer to God."

2. *The effective preacher conveys a lively interest in, and love for, the Scriptures.* Preaching has been described as a "breaking open" of the Word, a metaphor that harkens back to the Luke 24 story of the disciples on the road to Emmaus; as the Risen Christ broke bread with the confused disciples, he also "broke open" their understanding of the Scriptures. Within a few lines, the attentive hearer can tell whether the preacher has wrestled with the scriptural text out of an authentic love for the Word of God. The preacher not only has a message that matters, he conveys personal investment and a sense of urgency. All preaching involves personal witness. This does not mean the preacher talks about himself, but that his own faith and desire for deeper faith is on the line. He is preaching to himself as really as he is preaching to the congregation. Good preaching includes but goes beyond the past meaning(s) of a text and dares to suggest its meaning for us today. The preacher listens for the ancient meaning(s) but also listens for the text's possible meanings today, in order to provide what the US bishops called for:

. . . a scriptural interpretation of human existence which enables a
community to recognize God's active presence, to respond to that presence

---

11. *Deus Caritas Est*, 7.

in faith through liturgical word and gesture, and beyond the liturgical assembly, through a life lived in conformity with the gospel.[12]

3. *Good preaching inspires mission to others.* The effective preacher leads us to the Table and out the church doors through the parking lot to the world, where we serve our families, our places of employment, our society, our world. Effective preaching stimulates the will to do something with the message, to enact it in the challenges of daily life in all its various settings. One of the most profound compliments I ever received on my preaching came from a middle-aged man who stopped in the back of church one Sunday to say, "You know, Father, I listened to what you said last Sunday, and I went home and made up with my wife." Others have heard preaching that stimulated them to volunteer to teach catechism, ladle soup at the parish soup kitchen, run for the local school board, or get involved with an organization working for international economic justice. The Christian message is one of intimacy with God, but this intimacy is not purely inward looking; it clamors within us to be shared with others. The Sunday homily can be a means for strengthening and emboldening the community to give witness, serve unselfishly, and stand up for a more just world.

4. *Effective preaching is holistic: it deploys both discursive and imaginative language, and appeals to mind, heart, and will.* However theologically accurate it may be, preaching that is couched in purely discursive terms runs the risk of being received as abstract and dry. There are dimensions of the human personality that can only be reached and enlivened through the use of well-chosen imagery, metaphor, music, the arts, and story. Jesus himself was ingenious at this in his use of parables and in the most powerful narrative of all—his own life, suffering, death, and resurrection. Our faith rests on the paradox of the Paschal Mystery, and the preacher's task is to use all available means to help us find our true home there. It is that mystery that takes seriously, and sheds light upon, all human experience. If we aim for conversion and transformation of the whole person, then we need to appeal to both the "left brain" (rationality, logic, discursive language) and the "right brain" (image, story, intuition, creativity). And we need to heed the ancient advice of none other than

---

12. *Fulfilled in Your Hearing* (United States Catholic Conference, 1982), 29.

St. Augustine of Hippo, who counseled his clergy and catechists to teach, delight, and persuade or move to action,[13] reflecting an understanding of the human person as composed of mind, heart, and will.

5. *Effective preaching creates, nourishes, and calls others into Christian community.* Just as the Scriptures themselves are inherently communitarian, so good Catholic preaching avoids mere "me and Jesus" spirituality to open a life-giving vision of who we can be for one another, and who we can be together for others. The effective preacher is mindful of the ecclesial aspects of the text, and of the needs of the concrete community within which he speaks. He is sensitive to the shared life of his parish community, with all its joys and challenges, lights and shadows. His preaching suggests both personal and communal avenues of response to what God is saying. Community life itself is evangelizing and helps people toward Christian maturity in discipleship.

The astute preacher in an initiating parish will be aware of the many rich homiletic possibilities that come his way each week, not only in the Lectionary but in the rites themselves. While the Scriptures hold the central place in liturgical preaching, the ritual components may also be regarded as homiletic texts. This includes the various rites of the initiation process, from the Rite of Becoming Catechumens through the Easter Vigil. The texts, the gestures, the physical elements, and the people involved in the rites all present opportunities for preaching that can assist in deepening Christian discipleship. We will explore some of these homiletic opportunities in the chapters ahead. Moreover, even in the absence of a special initiation rite, the texts, gestures, physical elements, and participants in any ordinary parish Sunday liturgy present many possibilities themselves for homiletic reflection. Utilizing these symbolic and sacramental elements in preaching need not overshadow the biblical quality of preaching; indeed, preachers and faithful alike might be reminded that those very liturgical texts and elements are themselves rooted in scriptural narratives and injunctions. Good preaching often has a mystagogical quality, either foreground or background, retrospective or prospective.

---

13. See his *De Doctrina Cristiana* (*On Christian Doctrine*), especially Book IV.

Conclusion

A final consideration regards the scope of preaching in the parish. Flourishing parishes with robust evangelization efforts and initiation ministries thrive on a rich diet of the Word on many occasions and by multiple voices. The preaching at Sunday Mass has a certain pride of place, as part of the community's most important worship assembly. Yet the reservation of the liturgical homily to the priest or deacon does not constitute a monopoly on preaching. The Sunday eucharistic homily is a privileged moment within what should be a larger fabric of proclamation of the Word. The Church has always felt the need to hear the *kerygma* proclaimed and explained both inside and outside of the liturgy. One need only think of the first witnesses of the resurrection, the women who returned to the community to tell an improbable, amazing story. Think of the lay mendicants in the Middle Ages, or the legions of sisters and brothers who have taught and mentored the young in Catholic schools. Every age of the Church's life has been marked by a love for the Good News that overflows in a banquet of diverse celebrations and re-tellings of the story that brought the Church into existence. The wise priest or deacon preacher will learn to preach from the Sunday ambo in a way that animates and inspires others to preach in other ways: in catechesis, in accompaniment of the sick and suffering, in outreach efforts, even in the marketplace, factory, and office. In doing so, he will find that a richer and more variegated fabric of preaching in the community's life, far from detracting from his preaching ministry, actually increases interest in and attention to the Sunday homily. This provides the ordained minister with greater and more concrete support in his call to preach. Nothing improves the quality of preaching like the perception that preaching matters, that people are listening, eager, and acting upon what is said. The catechumens lead us here, too, for they are often among the most intent of listeners seated before us.

The Holy Spirit mysteriously works through us, our preaching, our communities, our service of others, and attracts others to our door. We turn our attention now to the first season of their journey, the Period of Evangelization.

Chapter Three

The Period of Inquiry, or Evangelization and Precatechumenate

But how can they call on him in whom they have not believed? And how can they believe in him of whom they have not heard? And how can they hear without someone to preach? And how can people preach unless they are sent? As it is written, "How beautiful are the feet of those who bring good news!" But not everyone has heeded the good news; for Isaiah says, "Lord, who has believed what was heard from us?" (Is 53:1). Thus faith comes from what is heard, and what is heard comes through the word of Christ.

Romans 10:14–17

The Precatechumenate: How Do They Find the Church?

The process by which people are drawn into faith, and into the initiation process, is ultimately mysterious. The Spirit of God works in various ways, many of them unseen, to draw people into the household of faith. For one inquirer, the journey may begin with an existential crisis; some difficulty, failure, or life puzzle arises, prompting searching questions for meaning that lead a person to look, or look again, at the responses to life's big questions given by Christian faith. For another, the entry may be communal; getting to know a Christian community in its joys and struggles, its virtues and way of life, perhaps through a spouse or friend or co-worker, intrigues a person to look more closely. For still another, the starting point may be a new level of personal unselfishness, one's own or witnessed in another, discovered through service of others or some form of social engagement; the realization of a kind of personal transcendence is both gratifying and opens horizons of new questions and new possibilities. At times, the invitation to a journey of faith, or to a new turn in that journey, seems to come out of the blue, inexplicably but with irresistible force. Yet wherever the path begins, explicit Christian witness plays a crucial role in the realization and solidification of faith, as St. Paul saw with great clarity and urgency. The quality of faith may precede and surpass the adequacy of words, and it is surely God's gift. But words mediate, clarify, deepen, and point to what God is doing in the soul. The Church, then, deliberately uses words to evoke the experience of God and the response of faith.

The text of the *Rite of Christian Initiation of Adults* is extremely brief on the Period of Evangelization and Precatechumenate. It introduces this period as "a time, of no fixed duration or structure, for inquiry and introduction to Gospel values, an opportunity for the beginnings of faith."[1] The absence of both a prescribed period and structure springs from a deep respect for the multitude of places and life situations from which inquirers come to us. People inquire when and as they are able, and may remain in this posture either briefly or for many years. Yet the text emphasizes that this period is "of great importance and as a rule should not be omitted" (RCIA, 36).

The Precatechumenate Process is Evangelization

As the text of the Rite indicates, the process is dialogical, driven mainly by the questions of the inquirers, which can range all over the map. But the Christian community through its representatives also speaks, providing an introduction to its core beliefs and values. This process of introduction is basic evangelization: "faithfully and constantly the living God is proclaimed and Jesus Christ whom he has sent for the salvation of all" (RCIA, 36). The text continues, "During this period, priests and deacons, catechists and other laypersons are to give the candidates a suitable explanation of the Gospel" (RCIA, 38). In addition, "opportunities should be provided for [inquirers] to meet

---

1. *The Rite of Christian Initiation of Adults, Study Edition,* (Chicago: Liturgy Training Publications, 1988), 14.

families and other groups of Christians" (RCIA, 38). The inquirers
will be best served at this stage not by formal programming, but by
informal opportunities to ask their questions and to experience
firsthand what the faith means in the lives of a variety of Christian
disciples. What I am envisioning here is not an extensive nor detailed
catechesis, but an invitation to consider the core *kerygma* of the Church's
faith in Jesus Christ, upon which all else depends. Thus, in the interplay of
questioning and shared witness, in the sustained conversation between
inquirer and community, the hope is that faith will begin to take root,
"so that the genuine will to follow Christ and seek baptism may
mature" (RCIA, 37).

Twice the RCIA text frames the goal of this period in terms of
conversion. The conversion sought here is a turning not only nor
primarily toward the Church, but toward the Lord (RCIA, 36). It is also
conversion of an "initial" kind. Initial conversion is then explained in a
twofold way—namely, to be "called away from sin and drawn into the
mystery of God's love" (RCIA, 37). Here the text is clearly shaped by the
Second Vatican Council, especially *Ad Gentes*, 13, which also speaks of
"initial conversion" that turns one from sin and toward God, "who
invites [the inquirers] to establish a personal relationship with him in
Christ." Both texts see this as the beginning of a "spiritual journey"
that leads into the catechumenate and beyond. "The candidates are to
receive help and attention so that with a purified and clearer intention
they may cooperate with God's grace" (RCIA, 38).

There is no liturgical celebration for entry into the Precatechumenate.
This is appropriately so, since Christian liturgy properly expresses
faith, while the inquirers are presumed to have no more than "a right
intention" (RCIA, 39.1). However, the text does not exclude the possibility
of some kind of public recognition of the presence of these inquirers,
who are also called "sympathizers." RCIA, 39.3, stresses that such an
occasion should be a context that "permits friendly conversation," but
may include the presentation of the inquirer by a friend and some word
or gesture of reception given by the priest or another representative of the
parish community. It is my impression that such semiformal public
moments seem to be qute rare in parishes today. Yet they could be
useful both for the inquirers and for the community, and potentially

could even be occasions for a brief, informal kind of evangelistic preaching. However, careful pastoral judgment based on the particular circumstances of the inquirers needs to be exercised. Some may not be ready for any degree of public limelight on their early journey, and no commitment should be solicited from any of the inquirers

The essential dynamics of the Precatechumenate, then, remain informal. Over-programming or over-structuring of this period might even work against the atmosphere of "friendly conversation" so important to these dynamics, which to tease out the inquirers' questions, longings, yearnings. Nonetheless, the evangelizing parish will want to consider carefully and deliberately how it is fulfilling its mission to invite others to taste the goodness we have found in Jesus Christ. A number of evangelization programs are on the market today. For a parish deciding to adopt such a program, one important and twofold consideration is whether the envisioned process (1) strikes the right balance between the inquirers' own initiative and agenda, on the one hand, and the Church's eagerness to share its foundational faith story, on the other, and (2) does so in a way that affirms and encourages active agency and personal seeking on the part of the inquirers. Although these two goals can sometimes seem to be in tension, they need not be in conflict. Indeed, in the process of evangelization we often discover that putting the inquirer's personal story in conversation with the Paschal Mystery releases unexpected insights and graces, as well as further and deeper questions. The very nature of Christian belief is that it sheds light on the unique path trod by each person, rescuing and healing the broken places, redirecting misplaced energies, providing new vistas of possibility for the person, elevating and illuminating that grace already at work in the person's life.

In addition to or within parish-wide evangelizing programs, the parish will want to provide low-key occasions for people to approach with their questions and curiosity. Many parishes, for example, regularly schedule "Come and See" gatherings, often after a Sunday liturgy in a church meeting room. These occasions work best if casually structured in an atmosphere of mutual dialogue. Done well, they have at least three advantages. First, a "Come and See" gathering, especially if accompanied by personal invitation, presents onlookers, "sympathizers," and the troubled with a concrete occasion and invitation to begin to seek what the Christian faith might hold for them. Second, such an occasion can be a way for the inquirer to hear a convincing message that the Christian community cares, that "we are here for *you*," not just to teach or persuade but to really listen—such a rare thing in our world today—and to offer support and assistance in any way the person might be in need. Third, while some who are of a more reticent nature may shy away from group settings, at least initially, for others there can be strength in numbers. As they meet other inquiring people, often with similar concerns and questions and life stories with many twists and turns, they may be emboldened to move forward in discovery.

Yet truly evangelizing parishes cultivate other ways in which to intentionally invite people. Again, personal invitation and accompaniment are key factors. For example, when parish potluck suppers, dances, or service projects are held, these are excellent opportunities for a no-pressure invitation to others to "come see what we are about" (or "come and meet new friends"). A friendly greeting by a minister of hospitality at the church door as people enter for Sunday Mass can make a huge difference—especially if the hospitality minister remembers names. Personal attention from a priest, deacon, lay ecclesial minister, coworker, neighbor, or youth minister, even if only momentary, may reduce the distance and difficulty for a person to approach more closely and be more open about his or her interest. Evangelizing parishes are also becoming more adept at using traditional media (radio and television) and digital platforms (e-mail, the parish website, social media, and the like) to hang out their shingle and attract the attention of seekers. Parishes with active social ministries and charitable programs often attract people who are looking for a friendly and supportive place to ask the searching questions they carry around.

Preaching for Evangelization

What is the preaching that leads and supports the parish's mission to evangelize? The fact is that, despite its prominence in the New Testament, and despite its prominence in our history (e.g., the missionary expansion in the Greco-Roman world, the mendicants of the thirteenth century, the missionary fervor of the Jesuits, Franciscans, and Dominicans in the modern era), evangelistic preaching is practically a thing unknown among Catholics in North America today. It is hard to find clear and successful examples to point to today. Perhaps we are overdue for a renewal of evangelizing efforts, including preaching.

Pope Paul VI actually called for such a renewal more than four decades ago. He described "evangelizing preaching" as

> . . . simple, clear, direct, well-adapted, profoundly dependent on Gospel teaching and faithful to the magisterium, animated by a balanced apostolic ardor coming from its own characteristic nature, full of hope, fostering belief, and productive of peace and unity. (EN, 43)

The pope's list of qualities may well characterize *all* good preaching, but clearly it has particular salience for preaching with an evangelistic aim. Simplicity, clarity, and directness will be especially important with hearers who have little prehistory with the Christian faith. Nonetheless, the preacher will want to avoid a condescending tone, treating the hearers like children or people with little sense or life experience. The "well-adapted" dimension of Paul VI's statement would seem to be a special reference to local conditions of culture, socioeconomic condition, educational level, and so forth. Like all preaching, preaching for evangelization will be grounded in the Gospel as interpreted by the Church's teaching authority. The "apostolic ardor" of the preacher is not an extra, optional ingredient, but an essential element and one that is closely linked with preaching's ability to nurture hope and faith, thereby bearing the fruits of peace and unity. The personal devotion of the preacher is not mere emotionality, but an obvious, deep-seated passion and urgency to share a message and a way of life that can make a crucial difference for the better in the lives of the hearers. Evangelizing preaching, whatever the source, stakes the speaker's personal witness to the Gospel to the effective delivery of that message.

Catholic preaching for evangelization will need to focus on the core *kerygma* of the Gospel and its meaning for our lives. How might we define that core proclamation? Here again reflection on the "hierarchy of truths" (UR, 11) in Christian faith will be important. Various ways of articulating this core for preaching might result. Michael Joncas says that "the preacher's evangelizing task is to proclaim Jesus as God's response to humanity's deepest longings,"

and "the preacher should stick to what is basic and distinctive in the
Christian worldview: the life, teaching, death and destiny of Jesus."[2]
The Lordship of Jesus Christ and the mystery of the Triune God are
certainly central to any understanding of the Christian message.
Clustered closely around those doctrinal affirmations are understand-
ings of the working of God's grace, the theological virtues, the way of
life implied in discipleship of Christ, the nature of sacraments, and
the meaning of church. All of these central mysteries have multiple
bases in the Bible. In short, evangelistic preaching can and should be
fundamental without being *fundamentalist* (the latter connoting some
form of biblical literalism, a narrow and closed theology, etc.).[3] More
importantly, the central proclamation of the Church is always Good
News, and thus the tone of preaching must always be positive, joyful,
hope-offering. This does not mean that it is devoid of challenge. The
moral challenges of discipleship can be made clear in preaching in a
direct fashion. However, the strength and power to meet those moral
challenges always flow from the Good News of God's gracious
encounter with human beings, a covenant relationship offered today
as surely as in the past.

The Sunday homily may not be the inquirers' first point of contact
with the Christian community and the Gospel, but for most it will be
a main source for understanding what the Church is all about. Those
who preach at the Sunday liturgy will need to be attuned and attentive
to the needs of such seekers. Priests and deacons may object that
preaching for evangelization on Sundays could "dumb down" the
homily, depriving the faithful who are far more advanced in the ways
of faith of an opportunity for deeper probing of the mysteries they
already know. Perhaps so. Catholic liturgical theology emphasizes that
the homily is fully embedded in, and integral to, the community's

---

2. Jan Michael Joncas, *Preaching the Rites of Christian Initiation* (Chicago: Liturgy Training
Publications, 1994), 25.

3. See James Dunning, *Echoing God's Word: Formation for Catechists and Homilists in a Catechumenal
Church* (Chicago: Liturgy Training Publications, 1993), 155–158.

worship, not an interruption or set apart from worship,[4] and thus assumes that the homily speaks from faith to faith. However, two other factors deserve consideration here. One is that our liturgical assemblies are already mixed—that is to say, they already contain seekers, sympathizers, potential or active inquirers, and often in greater numbers than we may realize. A pastor who really pays attention to his flock learns about them and their presence.

So preachers already face this problem of how to gear their remarks for widely varying faith levels and stances; proposing that Sunday homilists consider the needs of inquirers is not creating a new problem, but inviting attention to one that already exists.

Moreover, considering the needs of inquirers oversimplifies both the nature of the Sunday assembly, and the nature of faith itself, to categorize participants too summarily. None of us—however long we have been fully initiated Christians, or however seriously and intentionally we may have taken the spiritual journey—none of us outgrows the need to hear the Gospel message again and again and again. There is always more to learn about Jesus Christ, always shortcomings and blind spots in our discipleship to be overcome, always an invitation to grow into the person of Christ more fully ourselves. The structure of the liturgical cycle corroborates this permanent need of all the faithful to be reminded and challenged to re-appreciate and go still deeper into truths confronted many times before. The nature of the Eucharist, too, in which the Paschal Mystery —the core narrative of the *kerygma*—is announced, retold, and enacted again and again, further attests to the unchanging need of all the baptized to be nourished by the same old realities. So the homiletic needs of the "old hands" are not so radically different from those of the newcomers and first-time visitors. Through study, through paying close attention to life and listening deeply to his people, through years of observation and practice, a skilled homilist is able to grasp the

---

4. For example, *Sacrosanctum Concilium* said that the homily is "part of the liturgy itself" (SC, 52; see also SC, 35). This statement is quoted in *Fulfilled in Your Hearing*, 23: "A homily is not a talk given on the occasion of a liturgical celebration. It is 'a part of the liturgy itself.' In the Eucharistic celebration the homily points to the presence of God in people's lives and then leads a congregation into the Eucharist, providing, as it were, the motive for celebrating the Eucharist in this time and place."

fundamental unity of the human condition seated before him, while also knowing how to speak to these divergent but overlapping audiences in a single homily of unified theme.

The evangelizing preacher, however, will also bear in mind that truly effective preaching requires even more than a good and true message centered in the Gospel. With an eye on that central message, the preacher must then consider how best to help his hearers connect that message with their lives, incorporating it into their relationships with God and others and living it out in practice. In its 1982 document *Fulfilled in Your Hearing*, the Bishops' Committee on Priestly Life and Ministry makes the all-important point that "The homily is not so much *on* the Scriptures as it is *from* and *through* them," aiming at a "scriptural interpretation of human existence."[5] The scriptural message, in other words, becomes a lens through which the hearer is invited to see not only God but to see his or her own life and the world, as well. This is not a glib or superficial kind of "relevance" or "application" of the text to life, but rather a kind of vision in which the hearer will discover new possibilities for life, for intimacy with God, for service of others. A robust homiletic message provides the hearer with a new way to look at her or his life story, a new way to see the meaning of life and a new framework in which to interpret life's events, joys, challenges. Good preachers tackle this task zealously but respectfully, non-dictatorially. It is a challenge that requires at least as much diligence, creativity, and selflessness as the first task of discerning the day's central message. The preacher looks for ways to invite the individual hearer and the community collectively to step into the homily's point of view, try it on, and make their own discoveries. The homilist can and should assist with this process, using not only discursive language but image, metaphor, and story. He can suggest, illustrate, and exhort, but he cannot close the loop or make the personal interpretation too narrow, specific, or ironclad; he must deliberately leave something mysterious and open-ended, as work and prayer for the hearer to do. The preacher trusts the Holy Spirit to finish

---

5. Bishops' Committee on Priestly Life and Ministry, United States Conference of Catholic Bishops, *Fulfilled in Your Hearing* (Washington, DC: USCCB Publishing, 1982), 20 and 29, respectively.

the task, using the words of preaching but assisting the hearer in the intimate work of receiving, believing, and committing.

Moreover, the evangelizing preacher needs to consider carefully not only the rightness and trueness of the *kerygma* to be heralded, but also the ways in which his listeners actually hear and receive the message, come to faith in it, and commit their lives to its living. A good message poorly constructed or poorly delivered will fail in its mission of conversion. Discursive language can only appeal to the rational mind; preachers need also to appeal to the mediating capacities of image, story, and example. Good preaching appeals to the imagination, the heart, and the will, as well as to the cognitive intellect. A preacher whose manner and demeanor convey little sincerity or personal investment, or scant understanding of the challenges and longings of the lives before him, may be tolerated, but is unlikely to move his hearers to a meaningful consideration of what is at stake in the scriptural text. Effective evangelizing preaching deploys fresh language for ancient truths, and brings the hearer to the cusp of encounter with a living God.

In addition, evangelizing parishes need to guard against an insidious tendency toward exclusive reliance upon the parish priests and the Sunday homily to do the work of sharing the Gospel. The RCIA rightly envisions the proclamation of the Precatechumenate as largely informal and coming from a variety of people in the community. This is not to denigrate the clergy nor downplay the role of liturgical preaching. It is, rather, to acknowledge the power of honest, one-to-one conversation and the complementarity of voices that are lay and ordained, women and men, young and old, believers of various walks of life. While the pastor speaks from the Sunday ambo with a unique and authoritative voice, the friend, neighbor, or coworker speak from a kind of authority unique to them, as well. One of the challenges for the ordained preacher is to exercise his ministry in a way that stimulates others, by virtue of their Baptism, to give witness to Christ in their own personal way and in their own life contexts. This animation of lay witness is nowhere else as crucial as in the period of evangelization. Most catechumens begin their journey through an experience of faith shared by a non-professional member of the faith community. This is yet another reason for Sunday preachers to consistently shape their homiletic message in a way that is not purely a private matter, that is, "me and Jesus," but thoroughly ecclesial in character. The Scriptures are themselves intrinsically communal texts, and the task of interpretation must carefully take that communitarian outlook and dimension into consideration. The Sunday preacher will find many reasons to advert in an affirming way to the indispensable need for the gifts and roles of others in the community. Doing so will call forth the service of others, explicitly or implicitly.

Is all of this a tall order? Certainly! Let's take a look at one attempt to do it.

Homily ▪ Third Sunday of Ordinary Time, Cycle A
Isaiah 8:23—9:3 1 ▪ Corinthians 1:10–13, 17 ▪ Matthew 4:12–2
Michael E. Connors, CSC

Not long ago, I was watching a few minutes of a program on 9/11. I watched the events of that awful morning from the safety of television, as you probably did too. The program reminded me of how many things happened just in those first short hours during and after the attacks. People dropped what they were doing and fled the buildings. Brave firefighters and police dropped what they were doing and rushed *into* buildings to do their duty, many of them never to return. People on another airplane dropped their usual guardedness and fear and rushed their hijackers, losing their own lives but probably saving hundreds of others. Think of the many split-second decisions that had to be made, many of them decisions to turn away from fear or self-interest to pursue a greater good. What is it, I wonder, that supplies people with that kind of courage in moments of crisis?

Tonight's Gospel is one of those passages that suggests that Jesus had a similar kind of electrifying effect on people. The Gospels are filled with this sense of urgency that invites people to meet and follow Jesus. In response to Jesus' preaching, people not only felt something, they not only got an intellectual message, but they changed their lives, reordered their priorities, turning on a dime in a different direction in some instances. In today's text Jesus appears suddenly, issues a summons, and Peter and Andrew, James and John lay aside their nets to follow him. His very presence, his invitation to friendship and discipleship were enough to make people drop what they were doing, leave behind their careers and way of life, and set off in a direction where they had almost no idea where they were going. What kind of energy did he have that makes people behave that way? What was it about him that people sensed almost immediately?

Several years ago I was in New Orleans for a conference. On Sunday morning, a group of us attended Mass at St. Peter Claver Church, a black Catholic church in a rather run-down neighborhood. I have to tell you, from the moment we walked into that church I knew this was going to be something very different. The first thing that hits you is the gospel music: energizing, foot-stomping, hand-clapping, get-up-outta-your-seat songs with powerful rhythms that drew everyone in attendance into them. It has an uncanny way of overcoming resistance and gets you into it, whether you want to or not.

Then there was the preaching. It was in that interactive style so common in black churches. The deacon who preached elicited shouts of "Amen!" and applause. His message was simple, even though that homily went on far longer than this one will, and it was proclaimed in a way designed to hit you right between the eyes. It went something like this: "*Jesus* is the one! *He's* the one you've been looking for! *He's* the one who can turn the lights on in the darkness of your life! He is *The Man! Jesus* is the one! Amen!" About every other line of his was answered with cries of "Amen!" from the people.

Now, I don't know about you, but I need to hear a message like this once in a while. It reminds me of what is at stake here. It reminds me that following Jesus is not just a bunch of interesting or curious religious ideas, not just a nice thing to do on Sundays, and not just about eternity, but *a powerful force that saves us from things that could kill us.* It reminds me that without him as the light of my life things would be very dark indeed. And it shows us a whole way of life that indeed does ask us to drop what we were doing, leave other things behind, and set off in an entirely new direction.

Let his presence light you up, today and each day. Hear him say to you, "*You are mine, I will never abandon you.*" Drop what you're doing, today and each day, and turn in his direction. The magnetic, life-giving person of Jesus stands before us, interrupting our schedules, our routines, our plans and our expectations, with the simplest yet sweetest and most important message we will ever hear: *"Come after me."*

Commentary

This homily was not preached to a group of inquirers, nor with any identifiable inquirers present at all — but it probably could have been. It was preached on an ordinary Sunday evening to an assembly of college students, mostly Catholic, some of them deeply faithful, others intermittent in their practice or still wondering what it all means for them. It is not long — not because the preacher should be afraid to ask for time from these busy kids, but because an economy of well-chosen words is often the best approach to people who are drowning in words and concepts, people living in a world that is awash in words, concepts, marketing pitches, claims and counterclaims. People are sick of slick advertising that manipulates and even manufactures need. Innately they know that words that flatter and titillate, ooze with sweetness or browbeat with guilt, do not have the ring of authenticity. Speech that is direct and clear and to the point, and offers genuine encounter, wins a hearing. So the sentences here run straight and true, mostly avoiding long and compound construction, dependent clauses, exaggerated adjectives, glib or formulaic or esoteric religious language.

The structure or "form" of the homily is not complicated; it contains only four basic "moves" or parts, all converging on one unifying theme. This makes it easy to follow, and its fundamental message impossible to miss. The homily does not dwell overly long on the scriptural text, and yet it is infused with the Gospel story at hand. It does not distill a moral or message from the text, but seeks to draw the hearer into the text.

There is personal investment in this homily, a genuine *I* speaking. It is not an *I* who calls attention to himself, but one who also stands in need of the message, who stands consciously from and among the fellow hearers. There is revelation of shared human need, given voice in carefully phrased questions. The response to those questions is to point to a Christ who came to address real and pressing human need, not only in the distant past but also in the right here, today, now. The central focus is a living Christ in whose immediate presence we gather. It directs the hearers' attention to the electrifying effect that Jesus had on people, presenting and inviting, without demanding, that today's hearers can touch that presence too.

There is urgency in this homily too. The darkness and difficulty of life is not dwelt upon or exaggerated, but named frankly. Our very lives and well-being are at issue in how we respond to the invitation from Jesus. The theology of the homily walks a fine but crucial line, affirming that the initiative comes from Jesus, and everything depends upon him, while still valuing and urging our free response in faith. It leaves the hearer with a near-at-hand invitation. It is the goodness of the One who draws near that empowers the hearer to drop the lesser goods (and not-so-goods) already in hand. What is at stake is immediate and urgent, and our response can be no less immediate and urgent. Yet the leaving behind is not sad or burdensome, because it is for the sake of a new adventure with and into the person of Jesus.

Notice too that the appeal of the homily does not rest completely, nor even mostly, on abstract or discursive kind of language. The imagination is engaged in at least three places: in recalling the dramatic events of 9/11, in exploring the Gospel narrative, and in the storytelling of another worship and preaching experience. The hearer is implicitly invited to picture these events and worlds, and picture herself or himself on the road with Jesus too.

There is basic *kerygma* in this homily. Jesus is "the one you've been looking for . . . a powerful force that can save us from things that can kill us." Every single member of the assembly is united in human need, in facing threats to our well-being. There is a grounding assurance of Christ's love and faithful presence with us, never abandoning us in that human need. And this Jesus issues a resounding invitation to companionship, "Come after me." This basic message is one we never outgrow, no matter our age, condition in life, or spiritual maturity. It is a timeless, universal invitation to discipleship.

Some seekers will hear words from us that intrigue them. Some will find here the promise of healing or hope they've been yearning for. Some will find that their personal life stories are listened to and illuminated in this period, and make the decision to commit themselves to learn and follow the way of Christ, asking help from us on the road to full initiation through Baptism. These inquirers are ready for formal acceptance into the catechumenate.

Chapter Four

The Rite of Acceptance into the Order of Catechumens

[Candidates,] you have followed God's light and the way of the Gospel now lies open before you. Set your feet firmly on that path and acknowledge the living God, who truly speaks to everyone. Walk in the light of Christ and learn to trust in his wisdom. Commit your lives daily to his care, so that you may come to believe in him with all your heart. (RCIA, 52)
Lord, we have signed these catechumens with the sign of Christ's cross. Protect them by its power. . . . (RCIA, 57)

The first time I celebrated the Rite of Acceptance into the Order of Catechumens, I was a nervous wreck, and not just because I had been ordained only a few months. I was well aware that this Rite asks all participants to step out of their usual liturgical roles and spaces to do and say things that are quite out of the ordinary. Would I blow my lines, I wondered, lose my place, or forget where to stand? Would the members of the parish community leave the safe familiarity of their pews at the beginning of Mass and gather with the catechumens, sponsors, and RCIA team outside the church doors? What would the catechumens say when questioned about the desires that brought them to our doorstep? Would the sponsors be too timid to sign their candidates on various parts of their bodies with the Sign of the Cross? How would the catechumens receive this gesture? How would the rest of the community understand the meaning of what was going on? Would they find it hokey, artificial, awkward? Or would they play their role enthusiastically, and maybe in the process feel themselves called to spiritual renewal and deeper conversion?

I need not have worried. As I took the hands of the new catechumens and led them across the church threshold and up the center aisle, singing a song of joy and thanksgiving, I knew that something important was unfolding; I knew that catechumens, sponsors, and community all recognized it and were entering into the moment with solemnity and joy. Lively chatter and celebration after Mass confirmed that the liturgy had called forth something life-giving for all of us. From that day forward, the Rite of Acceptance became one of my favorite liturgical moments.

The Rite of Acceptance: What Is Happening?

The Rite of Acceptance into the Order of Catechumens is ordinarily the first public rite to be celebrated by aspiring initiands. The Period of Inquiry has a certain degree of informality to it, and it takes place not in secrecy, but largely out of the public eye, on the periphery of the community and with no definite commitment. With the Rite of Acceptance, however, an inquirer steps deliberately out of the shadows and into the public limelight, into the center of the Christian community, with a firm intention of commitment. By joining the ranks of the catechumens, a person says, "I share your faith and hope in Christ Jesus. I want to become a public member of this faith community through the sacraments of initiation. Train me in your way of life and help me reach that goal of full membership." The public, ritual nature of this Rite draws a sharp distinction between inquirer and catechumen. The RCIA itself acknowledges this when it asserts that if a catechumen dies, the liturgy of Christian burial is celebrated (RCIA, 47). The implication is that catechumens are true members of the household of faith, albeit junior or apprentice members.

The *Rite of Christian Initiation of Adults* attributes "the utmost importance" (RCIA, 41) to this rite, and for good reason. The Rite of Acceptance is dialogical; on the one hand, the candidates "declare their intention" of full membership, and the Church, on the other hand, "accepts" them into a publicly acknowledged "order" of pilgrims on the way to full initiation (RCIA, 41). For these men and women, the RCIA sees this as a solemn moment of great divine blessing, calling it a "first consecration by the Church" (RCIA, 41) of the candidates. The public nature of what is taking place is emphasized twice in this first paragraph on the Rite of Acceptance.

This Rite is not to be undertaken lightly by either the candidate or the Church. A candidate should be accepted as a catechumen only if "the beginnings of the spiritual life and the fundamentals of Christian teaching have taken root," giving "evidence of first faith" or "initial conversion" (RCIA, 42). The text elaborates on this by asking for "intention to change their lives and to enter into a relationship with God in Christ . . . evidence of the first stirrings of repentance, a start to the practice of calling upon God in prayer, a sense of the Church, and some experience of the company and spirit of Christians" (RCIA, 42). The emphasis here is on right intention and the beginnings of the disciple's life of grace. That intention calls for an extended period of deep formation.

Readiness for the Rite of Acceptance calls for careful discernment from the Church. A candidate should be accepted only after a period suited to each individual. Moreover, the Church must "evaluate" and even "purify" the "motives and dispositions" of each person (RCIA, 43). The RCIA foresees that this discernment will require the involvement of a number of people: "With the help of the sponsors, catechists, and deacons, parish priests (pastors) have the responsibility for judging the outward indications of such dispositions" (RCIA, 43). Those concerned with the initiation process often report that such discernment is a weighty and difficult responsibility, not least because it seems to put them in the uncomfortable position of judging the character and motives of others. Fortunately, our tradition contains some fabulous resources on the nature and practice of spiritual discernment (e.g., Ignatius of Loyola's *Spiritual Exercises*). Initiation leaders should glean the tradition's wisdom in order to approach their task with the sacred respect that it deserves.[1]

The RCIA presumes that the Rite of Acceptance will be celebrated multiple times in the course of a year. No fixed times are set; the decision is left to the local parish. The possibility of the Rite being celebrated

---

1. Some resources to recommend: Donna Steffen, SC, *Discerning Disciples: Listening for God's Voice in Christian Initiation*, rev. ed. (Chicago: Liturgy Training Publications, 2007); Henri Nouwen, with Michael J. Christensen and Rebecca J. Laird, *Discernment: Reading the Signs of Daily Life* (New York: HarperOne, 2015); Timothy M. Gallagher, OMV, *The Discernment of Spirits: An Ignatian Guide for Everyday Living* (New York: Crossroad, 2005).

outside of Sunday Mass is left open, though clearly the Sunday liturgy is held forth as the preferred option: "It is desirable that the entire Christian community or some part of it, consisting of friends and acquaintances, catechists and priests, take an active part in the celebration" (RCIA, 45). The presider at the Rite is a priest or deacon. The names of those accepted into the catechumenate are enrolled in a special "register."

The Rite of Acceptance creates a new relationship between the Church and the catechumen. The catechumens are "now part of the household of Christ," whom the Church "embraces as its own with a mother's love" (RCIA, 47). The Church will "nourish them with the word of God and sustain them by means of liturgical celebrations" (RCIA, 47). For their part, "the catechumens should be eager to take part in celebrations of the word of God and to receive blessings and other sacramentals" (RCIA, 47).

Examining the Parts of the Rite

The first and one of the most remarkable things about the Rite of Acceptance is that it is recommended to take place in an unusual setting: outside the church sanctuary, or at the church entrance. The RCIA envisions this as a procession of the faithful accompanied by the singing of a psalm or other music (RCIA, 48). The Christian community leaves its accustomed place and security and, as it were, moves outside of itself to greet the candidates. The presiding minister then "greets the candidates in a friendly manner. He speaks to them, their sponsors, and all present, pointing out the joy and happiness of the Church" (RCIA, 49). The dislocation of the community, and the face-to-face meeting with the candidates requesting initiation, is an occasion punctuated by joyful celebration. It suggests that both parties, the candidates and the Church, have moved from their familiar locations to this moment of encounter in a liminal space. Both the candidates and the community are under the leadership of God's Spirit, who prompts action and movement.

The presider then asks for the name of each candidate. This moment has a deep scriptural poignancy: the revelation of a name engages the whole of one's personhood and identity in this moment of commitment. In the biblical literature, giving the name grants access and intimacy with the one named. It acknowledges an existing relationship, or creates a new one marked by a particular kind of intimacy. The candidate is putting himself or herself on the line here, in the public eye, reaching out to the gathered community, and through them, reaching out to God.

The public proclamation of the name is followed by a second question, usually "What do you ask of God's Church?" Each candidate may give various appropriate answers, according to their personal journey and expression. The RCIA envisions responses like "Faith," "The grace of Christ," "Entrance into the Church," and "Eternal life" (RCIA, 50). The celebrant is then to probe the answer given further, with a third question, such as, "What does faith offer you?" A ritualization of the Church's evaluation of individual readiness is being played out here for all to witness. At the same time, the absence of a prescribed, uniform script is a gesture of the community's respect for the widely varying life paths that have brought these seekers to our doorstep. The community and its faith embrace all of those journeys, no matter where they began or where they have led. People come to Christ and to us for many reasons, with many needs and many gifts. We believe our faith honors, illuminates, purifies, and elevates all of our life stories, no matter their twists and turns.

The community's faith is then given voice in the next movement. Using one of three standard formularies (RCIA, 52), or adapting one according to the answers just received, the minister proclaims the central faith of the community in Christ, admonishing the candidates about what lies ahead as they share this faith. He then asks the candidate whether he or she is ready to accept and commit to that faith. The candidate must respond publicly, "I am." The minister then asks the sponsors and the whole community whether they are "ready to help these candidates find and follow Christ" (RCIA, 53). The assembly responds publicly, "We are." A covenant between catechumens and the Church has been struck. The presider solemnizes this covenantal moment with a prayer giving thanks and praise to God for the call given to the candidates, imploring God's help and protection.

What follows is one of the most striking series of ritual gestures in the Christian liturgical repertoire: the signing of the senses. The minister traces the Cross on the forehead of the catechumen, pointing to Christ as the source of our strength. In one of the available formularies he explains, "To admit you as catechumens I now mark you with the sign of Christ's cross" (RCIA, 55). Thus the signing is both a gesture of claiming the person for Christ, and an invitation to see life through our most potent sign of God's love. An admonishment to the candidate follows: "Learn to know him and follow him" (RCIA, 55). The celebrant also invites the sponsors and catechists to trace the mark of the Cross on the candidate's forehead, broadening the gesture to include others who are closely associated with the person's faith journey.

Optionally, seven more signings by the catechists or sponsors may then occur, to the ears, eyes, lips, heart, shoulders, hands, and feet. Each is accompanied by a ritual word that is part prayer, part invitation or admonition (e.g., "Receive the sign of the cross on your lips that you may respond to the word of God" [RCIA, 56]). The comprehensiveness of these eight signings should not be overlooked. We have before us, ritually enacted, a proclamation of the Gospel penetrating all of the senses and faculties of the human person, a visible, three-dimensional way of saying that Christ's power and life pattern shape our lives in every aspect and activity. It is a powerful, poignant moment of paschal faith.

After a closing prayer, the presider then invites the candidates and their sponsors to enter the church, "to share with us at the table of God's word" (RCIA, 60). It is desirable here that the minister takes the hands of the new catechumens and leads them up the center aisle into the midst of the assembly. The readings then proclaimed may be the Lectionary selections of that particular Sunday. The choice of a Sunday for the celebration of this rite is best done with some care, linking the rite to readings that reflect upon God's call and our response. Alternatively, the RCIA suggests two readings for this occasion; either or both may be used, supplanting the Lectionary readings of the day, if necessary. The first is Genesis 12:1–4a, the call of Abram to leave his country and go to a new land to be shown him by God.[2] The Gospel is John 1:35–42, in which two disciples of John the Baptist approach Jesus with questions, and Jesus responds, "Come, and you will see." These texts are particularly

---

2. This text also appears in the Lectionary for the Second Sunday of Lent, cycle A, where it is paired with the Matthew 17:1–9 account of the Transfiguration. Since the Lenten season has its own distinct purposes related to Initiation, this Sunday is probably not a good choice for the Rite of Acceptance.

well suited to the nature of what is happening in the Rite of Acceptance, and are generally preferred. The homilist then has the opportunity to unfold the connections of meaning for all present.

After the homily, the catechumens are remembered in the Universal Prayer, which is concluded with a special prayer over the catechumens, expressing the community's wish for their continued progress toward Baptism. The catechumens are then ordinarily dismissed kindly, before the eucharistic liturgy begins. One formulary says,

> My dear friends, this community now sends you forth to reflect more deeply upon the word of God which you have shared with us today. Be assured of our loving support and prayers for you. We look forward to the day when you will share fully in the Lord's Table. (RCIA, 67.B)

The presider should continue to dismiss the catechumens at this point at every liturgy they attend before their Baptism.[3]

Homiletic Possibilities in the Rite

How will you approach the veritable banquet of preaching possibilities in the Rite of Acceptance? Indeed, you will need to avoid the temptation to do too much, compromising that thematic unity which is so essential to preaching that is easily grasped and remembered. While the homily should always be scripturally infused, you will want to recall that the various rites, words, and gestures witnessed by the community can also be elements of reflection in the homily. As the homilist, you have before you a unique opportunity for a kind of mystagogical preaching, and this opportunity should not be neglected. Here is a brief sampling of the themes and connections that may be incorporated into a mystagogical homily.

---

3. The RCIA also includes the possibility of several additional parts to the Rite of Acceptance, at the discretion of the diocesan bishop. These include an exorcism and renunciation of false worship in place of the candidates' first acceptance of the Gospel (RCIA, 51); the giving of a new name (RCIA, 58); the presentation of a Cross or "some other symbolic act" that speaks to "reception into the community" (RCIA, 59); and the presentation of a Bible to the candidates (RCIA, 64). These do not seem to be in common usage in the US, and they should never be done in such a way as to eclipse the essential elements of the rite discussed here. Some of them might be usefully included among the many optional celebrations of the Word, which are envisioned to punctuate the whole period of the catechumenate. For a more detailed and wisely pastoral walk-through of the parts of the rite and the various options, see Paul Turner, *Celebrating Initiation: A Guide for Priests* (Schiller Park, IL: World Library Publications, 2007), 10–25.

Meeting the Catechumens at the Threshold

The *meeting outside of the church or at the church entrance* says a lot to all of us about the nature of being a Christian community and our evangelizing mission. As Church, we do not sit back comfortably in our pews; we process to or beyond the church doors, going out of our way to meet the new people who knock on our door, as it were. Just by their presence at our door, those candidates are a powerfully visible and multivalent sign to us. First, they are a sign of God's blessing to us in the gifts and personal life stories they bring to enrich our community. Each new member strengthens and enriches the community. Second, they are also a sign that reminds us that God is working among us, something any of us is apt to forget at times. The candidates desire to share in what we have—the goodness and challenge of our way of life as disciples—they see God among us, sometimes even more vividly than we do. Third, as the *catechumens are led across the threshold of the church*, they remind us that Christ invites each of us to proclaim publicly our hope in him, committing ourselves to walking with him, being formed by him, forsaking other life paths and trusting in him for all things. The homilist would do well to reflect the community's profound sense of humility and gratitude in the face of such unearned blessings and, consequently, its renewed resolve to follow Christ unreservedly. Finally, the location and movement of the rite, from outside into the church sanctuary, also provides an opportunity for you as the preacher or catechist to reflect with the entire community on the nature and crucial importance of hospitality to the stranger and the seeker. The homily on this occasion might well challenge the parish community to become more hospitable, especially through outreach to those in need. The evangelizing mission of Christ, in which we share, should cultivate in all of us an eagerness to meet people where they are and welcome them into the midst of our celebrations.

Dialogue with the Candidates

The *dialogue with the candidates* is striking not only for its very public character, but also for its directness and simplicity. As the candidates state their names, it ought to remind all of us that we are known and called, intimately and by name in all that that implies, by a loving and merciful God. It also reminds us of the revelation of the divine name in

Exodus 3:14, one of the pivot points of the fundamental narrative of Hebrew faith. In revealing the name, God has revealed God's very self to us, granted access to his presence and power, and pledged us an enduring covenant relationship that includes intimate, personal knowledge of God's very being.

Then the candidates go on record as seeking something, and it must be something of grave, life-defining import. While the answers of the candidates reflect their varying life stories and personalities, all of the responses point to something beyond ourselves, something to be touched only in God. Ultimately, only God can grant the requests of the candidates, and yet the candidates approach our community as the key to—one might even say, the sacrament of—those blessings. It is scarcely possible to overstate the honor they do us, although the preacher must be careful to emphasize that whatever the candidates seek from us, we can only give what we ourselves have received as gift. Thus, the community is not placed in a superior or condescending position vis-à-vis the candidates. Rather, we are joined together as companions on the road of discipleship, all the recipients of God's favor, which supplies our lives with meaning and purpose in ways we could not have generated ourselves. The approach of these candidates is cause for celebration, not triumphalism; for even greater humility, not braggadocio; for recommitment, not self-congratulation. The preacher or catechist will want to focus on God's action and goodness here, especially as they are enfleshed in the candidates and their desire to share more fully with us in the life of God. The homily may also take the question, "What do you ask of God's Church?" as a point of departure for reflection on our own lives. Although the question is asked explicitly of the candidates, it is asked implicitly of all of us, the baptized faithful no less than the candidates before us. What do we want? What are we really looking for? Good preaching arouses desire, thirst, and hunger for God and the fuller life God promises us. Following that desire leads one to deeper regions of the spiritual life.

First Acceptance of the Gospel

The *first acceptance of the Gospel* by the candidates comes in response to
a question from the minister. There are three forms of the question
(RCIA, 52):

> Are you prepared to begin this journey today under the guidance of Christ?
>
> Are you ready, with the help of God, to live this life?
>
> Is each of you ready to accept these teachings of the Gospel?

Any of the available forms, as well as their introductory sentences, could
be used homiletically, reshaped into a question for the whole community
that invites response, reflection, and recommitment.

Pledge of Support from the Community

The *affirmation and pledge of support by sponsors, catechists, and community*
is a brief but solemn moment in the rite, full of wider implications. What
kind of help will the candidates need? What does readiness to help on
the part of the community and its representatives actually mean? This
gesture invites reflection not only on what we are doing in this moment,
but on the very nature of being Christian community. The RCIA makes a
demand upon the whole community, and it is a demand that Christ and
his work should come first in our thoughts, efforts, and prayers. Our
pledge of assistance to the catechumens grows out of our shared consciousness of God's redeeming goodness, which first reached out to us.

The Signing of the Senses

The *signing of the senses* should never be abbreviated, because its spiritual
implications for all of us are so far-reaching. Who is this Christ whose
mind and way of life shapes not only our minds and hearts, but also the
way we perceive the world and engage in it? The gesture performed here
is not merely a sweet and pious wish for Christ's help. It is a very pointed
reminder that Christ's own fidelity to the Father and the way he lived
led him to crucifixion on Calvary. Thus our lives, too, will be cruciform,
following the dying-and-rising pattern of the Paschal Mystery that lies at
the very center of our faith. The signing invites us to ask ourselves how
deeply we believe in the Cross; and how generous we ourselves are in the
self-sacrificing, self-emptying love which marked the life of Christ.

The eight-fold nature of the signing should prompt us to ask ourselves probing questions about our own "yes" to Christ. We may well find, upon reflection, that we have allowed Christ to shape certain aspects of our lives, while withholding others. This part of the rite presents us with a full-orbed, holistic ideal of discipleship. Preaching about these gestures can help all of us take a moral and spiritual inventory and move toward greater integration of our faith into all parts of our lives.

Prayer for Protection and Perseverance

A presidential prayer for protection and perseverance of the candidates caps off the signing of the senses. Here, in either formulary, the emphasis is on the salvific power to be tapped in Christ's death and resurrection. The road of discipleship beckons before them, as it does for the rest of us. That road will have its challenges and pains. All of us depend upon God's grace to sustain us and guide us on the journey.

The Liturgy of the Word

Genesis 12:1-4a, while not required for the Rite of Acceptance, is linked with this rite for good reason. The call of Abram is one of many poignant and instructive covenantal call narratives in the Bible, but in a way it is the prototype because Abram, later to become Abraham, is the great ancestor in faith. The parallelism with the catechumens' story is striking. Like Abram, they are called to a journey of faith, a journey that will take them to a new place, a "foreign land," as it were, a new kind of life, which they cannot fully know before their arrival. As with other scriptural call stories, Abram's election by God carries with it (1) an *element of mystery*, in the designs of the divine elector, who is supremely free to choose and confer blessing; (2) *a command* to do something, go somewhere, respond in some public way; and (3) *a promise* of something far grander than anything humanly possible. Similarly, the catechumens have been mysteriously and freely chosen, commanded to pull up stakes and relocate their lives, with the promise of great blessing to come. Yet this is a true story for each of us in the Christian community, as you, the homilist, would do well to remind us. Our lives are mysteries of election, ongoing response and undeserved blessing. The catechumens' journey serves to remind us of the gratuitous nature of God's initiative toward us. Moreover, Abram's accompaniment by Lot and Sarai and others serves to remind us that our journey is always in the company of others. We are part of a pilgrim people, a community on the way.

John 1:35-42, also not required, continues the theme of call. Jesus' question, "What are you looking for?" has already been mirrored in the questioning of the catechumens outside the Church. It is, in a sense, *the* question for seekers becoming catechumens. John the Baptist's recognition of Jesus is mysterious, unexplained. It occasions Jesus' equally inexplicable call of the two disciples to "Come and see." In typically Johannine symbolic language, Jesus is inviting the two to discover more than his house, but rather where he lives most deeply, in the relationship with the Father that drives his preaching and healing mission to others. The two disciples enter the house of Jesus to be tutored in this way of life, much as our catechumens now cross the church's threshold to become apprentices in the Christian life. The two disciples, in turn, become evangelizers of others, including Simon, whose call is specially confirmed and celebrated by the giving of a new name, Cephas or Peter. Similarly, the catechumens will be made new by the presence and grace of Christ, and they too will bear witness to their families, friends, and coworkers. For all of us, relationship with Jesus Christ begins with his call to us to follow, listen, and learn, and his tutelage takes hold and ripens into spreading the Word to others. As a homilist, you may help us recall our own vocations, the permanence and graciousness of the call, and the ways in which God continues to reach out to us and invite ever new responses of faith. For all of us, catechumen and baptized alike, there is an element of blindness as to the exact destination to which we are called. The invitation is to proceed in trust on the confident foundation of God's promise.

The Dismissal

The *dismissal of the catechumens*, which takes place at the conclusion of the Liturgy of the Word on the occasion of the Rite of Acceptance and continues at subsequent liturgies until their Baptism, is sometimes reported to be puzzling or even jarring for the community. The qestion "Why do they have to leave?" is not infrequently evoked, sometimes coupled with the complaint that it seems inhospitable, especially after we have just accepted them into our community. There is, to be sure, a bit of tension between our ritual welcome of the catechumens at the door and this moment of bidding them a temporary farewell. The community needs to remember that since the catechumens are junior members and will not be admitted to the eucharistic table until they complete their initiation in Baptism, the dismissal should not be viewed as unwelcoming but as simply courteous. Since they cannot yet share at the family table, it is better that they leave the assembly to deepen their study of the Word of God, mentored by their catechists and sponsors. They are joined to us, really but incompletely. Together we look forward to the day when we will share fully not only the banquet of the Word, but also the banquet of Christ's Body and Blood. The departure of the catechumens and the questions this gesture provokes present the homilist and catechist with an opportunity to reflect upon the great riches we as baptized, fully initiated members share in the Eucharist. The question is not so much, "Why must those people leave?" as it is "Why do we get to stay? And what does this great privilege of sharing a meal with the Lord entail for us?" The dismissals often arouse in the catechumens an ever-deeper hunger to share in the Eucharist and in the full dignity of Baptism. Likewise, the homilist may point to the dismissal to whet the appetites of the fully initiated for greater re-appreciation of what we do in the sacrament.

Let's examine another sample homily.

Homily 1 ▪ Rite of Acceptance into the Order of Catechumens
Genesis 12:1–4 ▪ Psalm 33 ▪ John 1:35–42 ▪ Michael E. Connors, CSC

Several years ago, I took a group of students to Haiti. A couple of months before we went, I went down myself to spend a few days just seeing what we were getting into. Notre Dame has a very ambitious project going on in Haiti, spearheaded by one of my Holy Cross confreres. The goal is the elimination of a disease, lymphatic filariasis ("elephantiasis"), from the country. The terrible earthquake of 2010 had set things back, but the work continues.

On my scouting trip, I carried with me several questions, including a very basic one, "Why are we even doing this? What is the point of taking students to what is one of most difficult environments in world?" I could have given some good educational answers about how it's good for us to learn about the wider world and the Church, to study the issues in this poor, tiny country practically on our doorstep, and so on. And those goals are certainly worthy ones.

But I received an additional and unexpected answer from one of the Haitian program directors. He remarked to me, "Your visit is a boost for us, because it means you have enough confidence in our country and its future that you can come and we can talk together." I didn't immediately grasp the full import of what he was saying to me, that this was not just a polite throwaway line, but something he really felt from the heart. After all that troubled little country has been through, they are in need of some good news, and they find it in being honored by visitors from far away. Hospitality is among the highest of virtues in Haiti — just as it is, not coincidentally, in the Bible. In our dominant Anglo culture, I fear we have almost lost the sense of visitors being an honor to us. But in Haiti, as in much of the developing world, the act of opening one's door to receive a guest is a sacred duty, and one of life's great joys. So we went to Haiti to honor our brothers and sisters. In addition, we went to be honored by the presence of Christ in the Haitian people. I can tell you that trip had a profound effect on all the students, and on me too.

Friends, we are paid a great honor today that these candidates and other seekers like them have crossed the threshold of our community and joined us on the journey of faith, offering their lives in service. They could be doing something else with their lives. Each candidate and each catechumen who come to join us on the path of discipleship pays us a great honor. Each of them has heard a call like God's call to Abram, asking them to leave the familiar and journey to a new place of blessing. And today they cast aside fear to answer that call.

One thing is clear: we are not worthy of them. We may think that *we* have issued an invitation to "come and see" who we are and what we are about, and in a certain sense that is true. But the more important thing is that they have heard *Christ* say to them, "Come and see . . . come and see." Come and see us Catholics, how good and virtuous and generous we are? Not so much. Come and see the beauty of our churches, our way of life, our care for one another, our care for the poor? Still not enough.

Rather, come and see this mesmerizing, fascinating person of *Jesus*, whom we try—and often fail—to follow, the story of death giving way to resurrection that he wrote with his own blood, and traces even today in *our* blood. Come and see the joy and the challenge we find in Christ, the comforting and discomfiting truths he shows to us; the ways he walks with us, and the ways we walk in darkness, having to trust that he is still by our side. Come and see us sign our bodies (✛) each time we enter this or any church, not with a sign of power or triumph over others, but with the sign of power made visible in weakness and willingness to suffer. Come and see a passage through dangerous waters to something like new birth again and again and again. Come and see a banquet table that nourishes and sustains us, but that also leaves us hungry for justice and bread for all of God's people on this broken planet.

"Come and see." Cross this threshold if you dare to say *yes* to this, if you dare to say *yes* to making the cruciform pattern of life the one you want to be conformed to, in head, ears, eyes, lips, heart, shoulders, hands, and feet, imprinting itself on every aspect of our being: our work, our leisure, our study, our play, our relationships, our past and our future. "Come and see." Walk with us, and we will walk with you, as together we walk with Christ the road that leads to Jerusalem, to Calvary . . . and to the empty tomb.

Commentary

Clearly this is but one of many possible homiletic approaches to the occasion of the Rite of Acceptance. It attempts to center itself on the invitation of Christ, "Come and see," while avoiding the common pitfall of trying to do too much.

The homily begins from a rather striking recovery of the virtue of hospitality—in this case, the hospitality of the poor shown to us who are better off. It conveys that the candidates knocking on our door indeed do us a great honor, and one that should be met by our best efforts to be truly hospitable. Yet the object of their desire, and the initiator of the invitation to join, is not really us but Christ, who says to all, "Come and see." Thus, the catechumens are for us, the fully initiated, not cause for bragging but cause for celebration and humility. The catechumens are beginning to acknowledge a debt that is our debt too — a debt that we can never repay. We are neither spiritually nor morally superior to the catechumens, and it is good for us to be reminded of that as our apprentice members traverse toward full initiation. God entrusts these people to our care, which is an enormous privilege. However, here, as in all good Christian preaching, the emphasis is on God's free action preceding and underlying anything of value that we can do. None of the other actors — the candidates, the ordained ministers, the assembled faithful — are or will be doing anything as important and effective as what God has done, is doing, and will do. The repetition of Christ's "Come and see" invites all, catechumens and faithful, onto the road of continuing discipleship.

If the call is God's alone and completely gracious, it is nonetheless a call to a specific way of life, one deeply scored by the cruciform pattern of love we see most visibly in Christ's own story. Reflection on the eight-fold signing invites a most serious kind of catechesis on what it means to follow Jesus. On its own the Cross of Christ might not seem very appealing, linked as it is with suffering of a most cruel and grotesque kind. But the reminder here is that whatever suffering may be in store for us, it is only part of a larger narrative of suffering/death/resurrection. Just as God's call to Abram continues to resound in the call of these catechumens, so the promise given long ago to Abram still holds, and it is given special underlining in the death and resurrection of Christ. The destination is obscure, and the pathway's sufferings may even make that destination look dark and foreboding. We trust in a God of promise, whose Word is guaranteed by the astounding, unanticipated blessing of Christ's triumph over death and continued living presence with us in the Spirit.

This homily rings with invitation to respond. While some of these invitations are clearly directed to the catechumens, the entire assembly overhears and joins in the reception and the desire to respond. The Church is implicitly presented here not as a company of perfect disciples, but as a band of people still on the way, journeying together toward deeper fidelity and trust. We are on the way to Easter — not just in the coming spring but on the way to an eternal Easter of union with the Risen One. This gives us the courage, even eagerness, to embrace the Cross.

Homily 2 ▪ *Rite of Acceptance into the Catechumenate and Meeting with Catechumens at the Closing of the Year of Faith* ▪ Address of Pope Francis ▪ Vatican Basilica ▪ Saturday, November 23, 2013

Dear Catechumens,

This concluding moment of the Year of Faith sees you gathered here, with your catechists and family members, also representing many other men and women around the world who are in your same walk of faith. Spiritually, we are all connected at this moment. You come from many different countries, from different cultural traditions and experiences. Yet this evening we feel we have so many things in common among us. We especially have one: the desire for God. This desire is evoked by the words of the Psalmist: "As a hart longs for flowing streams, so longs my soul for thee, O God. My soul thirsts for God, for the living God. When shall I come and behold the face of God?" (Psalms 42 [41]: 1–2). It is so important to keep this desire alive, this longing to behold the Lord and to experience him, to experience his love, to experience his mercy! If one ceases to thirst for the living God, faith is in danger of becoming a habit, it risks being extinguished, like a fire that is not fed. It risks becoming "rancid," meaningless.

The Gospel account (cf. John 1:35–42) showed us John the Baptist who points out Jesus as the Lamb of God to his disciples. Two of them follow the Master, and then, in turn, become "mediators" who enable others to encounter the Lord, to know him and to follow him. There are three moments in this narrative that recall the experience of the catechumenate. First, there is the moment of *listening*. The two disciples listened to the witness of the Baptist. You too, dear Catechumens, have listened to those who have spoken to you about Jesus and suggested that you follow him by becoming his disciples through Baptism. Amid the din of many voices that echo around you and within you, you have listened and accepted the voice that points to Jesus as the One who can give full meaning to our life.

The second moment is the *encounter*. The two disciples encounter the Teacher and stay with him. After having encountered him, immediately they notice something new in their hearts: the need to transmit their joy to others, that they too may meet him. Andrew, in fact, meets his brother Simon and leads him to Jesus. What good it does us to meditate on this scene! It reminds us that God did not create us to be alone, closed in on ourselves, but in order to be able to encounter him and to open ourselves to encounter others. God first comes to each one of us; and this is marvelous! He comes to meet us! In the Bible God always appears as the one who takes the initiative in the encounter with man: it is he who seeks man, and usually he seeks him precisely while man is in the bitter and tragic moment of betraying God and fleeing from him. God does not wait in seeking him: he seeks him out immediately. He is a patient seeker, our Father! He goes before us and he waits for us always. He never tires of waiting for us, he is never far from us, but he has the patience to wait for the best moment to meet each one of us. And when the encounter happens, it is never rushed, because God wants to remain at length with us to sustain us, to console us, to give us his joy. God hastens to meet us, but he never rushes to leave us. He stays with us. As we long for him and desire him, so he too desires to be with us, that we may belong to him, we are his "belonging," we are his creatures. He, too, we can say, thirsts for us, to meet us. Our God is thirsty for us. And this is God's heart. It is so beautiful to hear this.

The last part of the narrative is *walking.* The two disciples walk toward Jesus and then walk a stretch of the road together with him. It is an important teaching for us all. Faith is a walk with Jesus. Remember this always: faith is walking with Jesus; and it is a walk that lasts a lifetime. At the end there shall be the definitive encounter. Certainly, at some moments on the journey we feel tired and confused. But the faith gives us the certainty of Jesus' constant presence in every situation, even the most painful or difficult to understand. We are called to walk in order to enter ever more deeply into the mystery of the love of God, which reigns over us and permits us to live in serenity and hope.

Dear catechumens, today you begin the journey of the catechumenate. My wish for you is to follow it with joy, sure of the entire Church's support, who is watching over you with great trust. May Mary, the perfect disciple, accompany you: it is beautiful to have her as our Mother in faith! I invite you to guard the enthusiasm of that first moment in which he opened your eyes to the light of faith; to remember, like the beloved disciple, the day, the hour in which for the first time you stayed with Jesus, felt his gaze upon you. Never forget the gaze of

Jesus upon you; upon you, upon you . . . never forget his gaze! It is a gaze of love. And thus you shall be forever certain of the Lord's faithful love. He is faithful. Be assured: he will never betray you!

Commentary

For those of us committed to the renewal of preaching in the Catholic Church, Pope Francis has been a great gift, both in his writings (especially *Evangelii Gaudium*) and in his personal example of preaching. This lovely little homily on the occasion of the Rite of Acceptance is a good example of his style of preaching, which is consistently touching, clear, direct. In the first movement, the pope unites himself and the whole Church with the catechumens, stressing all that we have in common, and especially a desire for God. This is not only a rhetorical act of hospitality; it also makes the homily an address to all gathered at this moment, as it should be. Both the baptized and the new catechumens are fundamentally one on the journey in their shared desire for God and God's life. Thus, while the homily is formally addressed to the catechumens, it is also effective for the wider community.

Francis then gently plucks three simple but powerful verbs from the day's Gospel reading: listening, encountering, and walking. Preachers will often do well to pay special attention to the verbs in scriptural text, for often they hold the key to the passage's meaning and dynamism. In this case, these three movements go right to the heart of the Christian way of life, which the catechumens are now setting out to learn. We listen to the Lord speak—the initiative is always his. We meet Him—the Christian way is about an encounter with a living person who is full of love for us. We then follow, walking the way with him and with one another. As we do, our lives are changed, transformed, given new meaning and purpose. The language of this homily is Christocentric, beautifully simple yet deep, relational, and dynamic. It engages not only cognition, but affect and will, as well. For both catechumens and faithful, this homily is a great gift of encouragement for those on the pilgrim way. One gets the sense that the speaker looks forward, with all the hearers, to the completion of this journey.

Propelled by the Rite of Acceptance, which celebrates their initial turn to Christ and desire for deeper faith in the midst of the Christian community, the catechumens set out on their journey through the period of the Catechumenate. The treasures of the Christian way of life await them.

Chapter 5

The Catechumenate

The homily can actually be an intense and happy experience of the Spirit,
a consoling encounter with God's word, a constant source of renewal
and growth.

Pope Francis, *Evangelii Gaudium*, 135

Formation and Transformation

Fifty years ago, in the aftermath of the Second Vatican Council,
Rosemary Haughton published her widely acclaimed book, *The
Transformation of Man*.[1] Haughton insightfully explored two great
dynamics at work in Christian faith. The first she called *formation*, a
word drawn from centuries of reflection on the process by which new
members are prepared for life in a vowed religious community or
membership in the clergy. Haughton described formation this way:

> The ideal of the formation of man is the process of using all the influences
> of culture—family affection, humane educational and political and social
> structures, and all the scientific know-how available—to help people to
> understand themselves and each other and the world they share, to adjust
> themselves to both without either undue aggressiveness or frightened
> conformity, and so to form satisfying and stable emotional and social
> relationships. This is to be done through a well-ordered community setting
> in which mutual responsibility and the care of the weak are taken for
> granted. All this, ideally, should produce the whole human being, the
> perfection of man. Nobody expects perfection in practice, but it is an
> imaginable ideal all the same, and one that seems worth striving for

---

1. Rosemary Haughton, *The Transformation of Man* (Springfield, IL: Templegate, 1967). In a 1980
preface to a new edition of the book, Haughton acknowledges a new sensitivity to the exclusive
use of *man* as a collective term for humanity.

because even its imperfect attainment produces a verifiable amount of human happiness.[2]

Formation represents the ordinary processes by which people are trained, educated, and equipped for life in a particular community. It thus includes most of what we Western Christians have generally called *catechesis* in the faith, usually directed toward the young. We can also think of formation as a kind of linear or organic growth process.

Haughton, however, identified a second dynamic, one that is much less under our control. This she called *transformation*, and she described it this way:

> But there is another notion of the purpose or perfection of man—the idea of transformation. It is not imaginable at all, which is why we tend to place transformed man in a separate "place" called heaven. Transformation is a total personal revolution. It begins with repentance—the rejection along with actual sins of the whole apparatus of natural virtue as irrelevant and misleading—and proceeds eventually to the desired dissolution of all that ordinary people ordinarily value in themselves or others. The result of this dissolution, this death of the natural man, is the birth of the whole human being, the perfection of man, meaning both man as an individual and man as a race, because the process is at once personal and communal. And it takes place in Christ and nowhere else. It is what Christians call the resurrection, or eternal life.[3]

Other terms for transformation are *conversion*, or in New Testament Greek, *metanoia*. When using this term, we can think of personal growth as interruptive, proceeding by jumps of insight, grace, and personal decision.

Haughton notes that Catholic Christianity has tended to place great emphasis on the former (formation), while the traditions flowing from the Reformation have tended to emphasize the latter (transformation). In her book then, she explores the interplay between these two dynamics. Her basic claim is that formation and transformation are not opposed, but yoked together. Formation, she believes, can be constructed in ways that seem to obviate the need for transformation, and may even work against it. For example, if a catechist reduces catechesis to indoctrination, mere mastery of doctrinal or catechism formulations

---

2. Haughton, *The Transformation of Man*, 7.
3. Haughton, *The Transformation of Man*, 7f.

without personal appropriation and deep, prayerful interiorization, then the promise of real transformation will be blocked, and the spiritual journey will be truncated. In other words, it is possible for formation to inculcate certain habits of mind and religious practice without authentic change of heart, vision of life, or behavior outside of church. Then the larger relational goals of catechesis—in particular, a living spirituality as intimate relationship with the divine—have been missed. However, formation can and should be arranged in a way that makes transformation or conversion more available, more likely to occur. In my experience, when we let the formation agenda for the catechumens flow naturally out of the Sunday Lectionary readings, and when we provided the catechumens with ample time and resources for personal reflection, meditation, group discussion, and prayer, then the catechumens' familiarity with doctrinal truth took on its rightful, three-dimensional character embedded within the life stories of each individual and could be powerfully transformative.

While formation can present a person with horizons of possibility, it cannot coerce people to cross into them. Conversion, in other words, is ultimately God's work alone. However, we can provide the kind of formative, catechetical experiences that will assist the catechumens in trusting God and yielding to the work of the Holy Spirit.

The Period of the Catechumenate

The *Rite of Christian Initiation of Adults* describes the catechumenate as "an extended period during which the candidates are given suitable pastoral formation and guidance, aimed at training them in the Christian life" (RCIA, 75). In other words, the catechumenate is a period of formation, a language the text picks up in the following paragraph when it says, "By their formation in the entire Christian life and a sufficiently prolonged probation the catechumens are properly initiated into the mysteries of salvation and the practice of an evangelical way of life" (RCIA, 76). The text reiterates that this formation takes a substantial period, "several years if necessary" (RCIA, 76).

However, the RCIA makes clear that the instruction and "practice" of this period are not ends unto themselves, but rather are ordered toward transformation. The aim is more than "acquaintance with dogmas and precepts"; it also includes "a profound sense of the mystery of salvation in which [the candidates] desire to participate" (RCIA, 75.1). The text describes this hoped-for transformation as "a progressive change of outlook and conduct" manifested in "social consequences" (RCIA, 75.2). The purpose is "for the conversion and faith of the catechumens to become strong" (RCIA, 76).

The fullest explication of the catechumenate's goal comes in RCIA, 78:

> The instruction that the catechumens receive during this period should be of a kind that while presenting Catholic teaching in its entirety also enlightens faith, directs the heart toward God, fosters participation in the liturgy, inspires apostolic activity, and nurtures a life completely in accord with the spirit of Christ.

This paragraph brings into focus the holistic aim of the catechumenate. There is an echo here of patristic sources, especially Augustine's *De Doctrina Christiana* (*On Christian Teaching*), in which Augustine says that the goal of Christian teaching is "to teach, to delight, and to persuade,"[4] or move to action. Augustine is relying on an understanding of the human being as composed of mind, heart, and will, an anthropology that he inherited from Cicero, the master rhetorician, who in turn got it from Aristotle. Paragraph 78 presents a picture of conversion in all three areas, integrated with one another.

Other sources can deepen and broaden our understanding of the conversion we are seeking for the catechumens. For example, one could study St. Paul's oft-repeated mantra, "in Christ," which he uses to unfold the multiple implications of converted discipleship in the life of the believer. Of particular note in the postconciliar era is Bernard Lonergan's differentiation of levels of conversion into intellectual, moral, and religious conversions.[5] Lonergan's pathbreaking work has been picked up by James Dunning and others, especially in the field of contemporary catechesis.[6]

---

4. Augustine of Hippo, *De Doctrina Christiana* (*On Christian Teaching*), Book IV, chapter 12, no. 27. (Oxford: Oxford University Press, 1995).

5. See Bernard Lonergan, "Dimensions of Conversion," in his *Method in Theology* (New York: Herder & Herder, 1972), 237–243.

6. James Dunning, *Echoing God's Word: Formation for Catechists and Homilists in a Catechumenal Church* (Chicago: Liturgy Training Publications, 1993). See also, Walter E. Conn, ed., *Conversion: Perspectives on Personal and Social Transformation* (New York: Alba House, 1978).

In sum, then, the catechumenate is *an extended period of formation in view of transformation*; that is, it is aimed at a wholistic and ongoing, lifelong process of conversion or deepening faith. The catechumenate's methods, then, must be similarly wholistic and integrated. The subparagraphs of Paragraph 75 provide a vision of such a comprehensive formation.

75.1 focuses on the *kerygma*, the proclamation of the Gospel that forms the core of the catechesis that the catechumens are to receive. The RCIA text says that this catechesis is provided by various representatives of the community, and that it is "gradual" and "complete." It immediately ties the catechesis to the rhythm of the liturgical year and to various "celebrations of the word." The goal is more than cognitive knowledge; it is *participation* in the mysteries.

75.2 is built on the principle of *koinonia*, or the importance of community life. The "example and support" of people in various roles, and of the whole community, are important to the formation of the catechumens. Mentorship is a key underlying principle in the understanding of formation running through the RCIA. The "spiritual journey" upon which the catechumens have embarked is not purely private, but is in company with a whole community—just as it is essentially communal in nature for all of us.

75.3 stresses the role of *leitourgia* or communal worship experiences of various kinds. The RCIA assumes that God speaks and acts through liturgy, and that liturgy, done well, has enormous formative power. The catechesis of the catechumenal period is not only a *study* of the word, it is an efficacious *praying* of the word.

Last but not least, 75.4 recalls that the essential nature of the Church is also *diakonia*, apostolic, and oriented toward active service of others. The Gospel is spread and witness to the faith is given through lives lived in unselfish love of others. Many would also attest that the faith is learned at levels of unique depth in the doing of it, through forms of service that are formative of the wills and habits of the participants.

The Role of Doctrine[7]

An understanding of the catechumenate as an extended period of
formation leads to the question of the role of Christian doctrine in
catechumenal catechesis. Without question, the Church's doctrinal
tradition is one of its great strengths. In every age the doctrinal heritage
has contributed to the Church's viability, fidelity, and adaptability.
The emergence of doctrinal formulations in the Church's early centuries
was closely wedded to the exigencies of preaching, catechesis, and
apologetics. Amid many and diverse challenges, there were pressing
needs to think through clearly the meaning of the faith and its
implications for Christian living.

Authoritative doctrine and magisterial teaching, then, have
served two broad purposes for the Church. One is to define what is out
of bounds, interpretations that lead in directions deemed erroneous or
incomplete. This function of doctrine is the more widely known one,
and yet it is quite rare for the Church to declare something heretical,
or out of bounds. The second, and perhaps even more important
though less well-appreciated function of doctrine, is to incite deeper
probing through faithful intellectual inquiry and prayer. Doctrine is
meant, for example, to push preachers into deeper water, away from
light or superficial readings of Scripture and toward the avenues of
authentic experience of the divine. Doctrine, while it is the product of
theological reflection, has also served to generate more theological
reflection. The nature of doctrinal language is highly compressed,
inviting the hearer to decompress or unfold it, and ask ongoing
questions of the doctrine's meaning, its relationship to other doctrinal
affirmations, and its relationship to the living of faith in every context.
Doctrine springs from the very nature of biblical faith, which is not a
closed or static certainty, but an ongoing and restless attention to a
dynamic relationship. One might say that doctrine attests to the power
of Christian truth to fire the mind, to arouse and direct the mind's
native inquisitiveness. The doctrinal heritage says to the believer, in

---

7. For a more thorough discussion of this topic, see Michael E. Connors and Ann M. Garrido,
"Doctrinal and Catechetical Preaching," in Edward Foley, ed., *A Handbook for Catholic Preaching*
(Collegeville, MN: Liturgical Press, 2016),124–133.

effect, "Keep probing, keep praying, go deeper into the inexhaustible mystery of a merciful God."

The compressed and abstract nature of typical doctrinal language, while it has the virtues of brevity and transportability, sometimes leads to misunderstandings of that language's message and purpose. Doctrinal language leaves much work for the end user to do, and this includes preachers, catechists, and ordinary believers. Patristic scholar John Cavadini says a doctrine is like a "little suitcase" or "carrying case,"[8] which has to be opened and unpacked. Another analogy might be to think of doctrines as being like "zip" files, highly compressed electronic files that have to "unzipped" by the user in order to do their work. Once unzipped, they set up whole programs—whole new worlds of thought and discovery for us. As Cavadini says,

> The teaching of doctrine often gets a bad name because we conceive of it not as the handing on of formative mysteries, but as simply informative, as merely informational. How often have you heard the phrase, "we have to get beyond the 'mere' teaching of doctrine"? In other words, to the real stuff, the experience, relevance, etc. The hidden premise behind this sentence is that doctrine is mere information and not in some way itself formation. What I say is, we have to get beyond the teaching of doctrine as though it were mere information.[9]

In the context of catechesis, doctrine can sometimes be undervalued or even dismissed. Too often, some regard it is as irrelevant, an erudite but abstract product of a bygone era with no meaning for life today. The result of this view can be an approach to catechesis that is superficial and that fails to introduce people fully into the treasury of Christian reflection on the meaning of Jesus Christ. However, by the same token, doctrine can also be overvalued, or *mis*valued. The ability to quote doctrine, Scripture, or patristic sources does not by itself make for effective catechesis insofar as the goal of that catechesis is the opening to total transformation. Sadly, doctrine and catechism have at times been used to close off discussion or further reflection rather than encourage and open it. The catechist or preacher still has the responsibility for unfolding the doctrine and its meaning for the hearer to grasp in

---

8. John C. Cavadini, "On Teaching Christianity," *Church Life* 1, no. 2 (2012): 26.
9. Cavadini, "On Teaching Christianity," 27.

multiple dimensions of human living. Both good catechesis and good preaching are doctrinally informed or infused. In general, that means that the doctrinal formulations themselves remain in the background, yielding to fuller and more immediate explanations of their meaning and relevance. The aim is for preaching and catechesis with substance and depth, and with visible, practical bridges into the lives people lead today, and the possibility for deep intimacy with God in those lives.

Preaching and the Catechumenate

What might all of this mean for preaching, if preaching is to benefit not only the catechumens but the whole assembly? A couple of preliminary points are in order.

Firstly, even when there are catechumens present at the liturgy, it is not necessary to preach specially to them. They are part of the larger assembly, and ordinarily the homilist should speak to the whole gathering. The catechumens are junior members of the Church in training, and they are invited to be part of the Liturgy of the Word celebrated by all. It is possible, even advisable, on an occasional basis to refer to them explicitly and speak a word specially directed to them and their needs. However, to some extent they are also learning and growing in the faith by *overhearing* the homiletic conversation between God and God's people, a conversation mediated by the homilist. The catechumens are in a liminal space, and the Liturgy of the Word is likely to evoke questions of meaning for them on any given Sunday. These questions should then be addressed in the "breaking open the Word" catechetical session that should immediately follow the dismissal of the catechumens from the liturgical assembly.

Secondly, we should bear in mind that while the catechumens have some formational needs peculiar to them, and while it is important to keep those formational needs in mind as we prepare to preach, the nature of their needs is not radically different from the needs of the rest of us in the pews. Like us, the catechumens are looking for meaning in their lives and striving to understand more deeply what it means to live in the light afforded by the Gospel. Like the catechumens, we who are fully initiated come to the liturgy with hopes, unfulfilled longings, sufferings, as well as joys and gratitude. After all, there is as much or more diversity among us who are fully initiated as there is between catechumens and faithful! As we fill the pews, our needs and hopes are not fundamentally of a different order from theirs.

Attending the Liturgy of the Word through a complete liturgical cycle or more, the catechumens undoubtedly will hear doctrinal and spiritual truths that are new to them. But the nature of these truths is such that even the oldest and most deeply committed disciples in the assembly need to hear them again and probe them more and more deeply. Who can ever fully plumb the Easter mystery of redemption? Indeed, every Eucharistic Prayer at every Mass retells the same old familiar narrative of Christ's death and resurrection, beckoning us into the story that is ever old yet ever new. Every Christmas retells the story of the Savior's coming among us, not to mention the multitude of ways in which the incarnation's meaning and implications are unfolded elsewhere in the Lectionary selections. The Christian life depends upon *anamnesis*, the exercise of sacred memory. For all of us, the Christian life remains a journey of discovery, not an arrival.

Most importantly, *the needs of both catechumens and the wider community will be well served if the homilist preaches wholistically, aiming at wholistic conversion.*

We have already explored the meaning of wholistic conversion as reflected in the text of the Rite. It is coded in terms like "participation in the mystery" (RCIA, 75.1), and especially in the various phrases of paragraph 78, as quoted above. However, what does it mean to preach wholistically, aiming to engender such wholistic conversion? Here we can only hazard a few basic thoughts on what is surely a very large and important topic.

First, we would do well to recall our friend St. Augustine's sage advice that preaching should teach, delight, and persuade (or move to action). In other words, both good preaching and good catechesis *appeal to the mind, the heart, and the will.* Homilists would do well to hold themselves strictly accountable to this triumvirate. Does the homily have a serious, substantive point, one that engages the intellect and invites continued, probing reflection? Is this message or theme presented with heart appeal, stirring the deep emotions or passions, inviting the hearer to fall in love with God and the ways of God? Finally, does the message move the hearer to response, commitment, and action, to do something with the message and to become something more? Wholistic appeal in preaching awakens and engages all three faculties, and in roughly equal measure.

Another important test for wholism is usually referred to as "right brain" and "left brain." The language in which preaching speaks should not be purely rational or discursive, but should also employ *image, metaphor, story, and even music*. The heart and will aspects of the human personality can only be effectively reached if one abandons exclusive reliance on discursive language and resorts to a rich banquet of imagery and narrative. As attested by the literature of the Bible itself, image and narrative have unique power to move and shape human consciousness and human living. The truths conveyed by these means cannot be "translated" into discursive language without a flattening in which something profound is lost. Preaching should employ the literary strategies that the genius of the biblical literature itself uses.

Wholistic preaching in the Catholic community must also be thoroughly *incarnational* in character. This means that it will strive to balance abstraction with concreteness. The preacher must name human reality as we actually recognize it to be: sometimes dark, perplexing, painful, challenging. Hearers are encouraged to hear the full scope of their lived reality named from the pulpit; doing so implicitly emphasizes that the good news being proclaimed is meant to land exactly there. All of human life and indeed the entire material world, is embraced, affirmed, and elevated in the message of the Gospel. Moreover, incarnational preaching conveys to the listener an important clue to the normal way in which God works—in the words of St. Thomas Aquinas, "grace builds on nature." That is to say, God ordinarily works through human beings, through the natural world, and through history.

Thus, the preacher is pointing to a spiritual doorway and inviting the listener to walk through it. Good preaching in a wholistic key is thus *preaching for the encounter with the divine*. The preacher is a mediator of meaning, facilitating a conversation between God and God's people. As Pope Francis says:

> The preacher has the wonderful but difficult task of joining loving hearts, the hearts of the Lord and his people. The dialogue between God and his

people further strengthens the covenant between them and consolidates the bond of charity. In the course of the homily, the hearts of believers keep silence and allow God to speak. The Lord and his people speak to one another in a thousand ways directly, without intermediaries. But in the homily they want someone to serve as an instrument and to express their feelings in such a way that afterwards, each one may choose how he or she will continue the conversation. (EG, 1430)

Preaching, therefore, is an exercise of the ministry of spiritual leadership. The homilist wants, above all, to lead the hearer into a meeting with the living God. The highest purpose of preaching is to assist people to encounter this God reaching out to us now, inviting us to life, to commitment, to discipleship, to transformation. The language that best makes this encounter happen is less like an academic theological lecture and more like the language of spirituality found in the writings of the saints and spiritual masters. That language is direct and immediate; it has a richly, vividly relational quality to it. Often this is the language of personal witness, either the homilist's witness or that of someone else or of the biblical author. The language of encounter addresses the question that hearers carry around with them as human beings and bring with them into the assembly: *How do I find God?*

Finally, the preacher should bear in mind the four dimensions of church in RCIA paragraph 75 we have explored above: *kerygma*, *koinonia*, *leitourgia*, and *diakonia*. While it is certainly not the Church that the homilist preaches, this fourfold understanding of the Church's nature and mission mirrors a total understanding of the mission of Christ himself. On the face of things, it may seem that preaching belongs only to *kerygma*, proclamation; this, however, is too narrow a view. Preaching, especially liturgical preaching, is not an isolated event but resides within a web of pastoral responsibilities and ecclesial activities. The homilist should take care to see that it is a proclamation, which works in tandem with care for community, the worship of God, and service of others. The preacher can model from the ambo an integrated understanding of these dimensions all working together to deepen and strengthen conversion for all in the community. Good preaching announces the Good News as clearly and powerfully as possible, and it does so, in part, by intentionally fostering communal bonds, raising hearts and minds to awareness and praise of God, and stimulating active love both within the community and beyond it, in the wider world.

Homily 1 • Feast of the Holy Trinity, Year B
Deuteronomy 4:32–34, 39–40 • Romans 8:14–17 • Matthew 28:16–20
Michael E. Connors, CSC

My alma mater is a small midwestern liberal arts college. Its lovely campus sits on top of a gently sloping hill. At the highest point of that rise, in the center of campus, is a spot that all of us alums claim as our own. There stands an enormous old oak tree, and from a huge branch a couple of stories up is suspended a swing. Beneath the swing, amid the roots of that old tree, are two deep ruts where thousands of feet have worn the earth smooth. I don't get back there too often now, but when I do, I of course have to sit on that swing, drag my feet through those ruts, and gaze out upon the largely unchanged landscape of buildings and walkways where I spent four of the most important years of my life. It always amazes me how simply being in that spot for a few minutes brings back a flood of memories: things I did in those years, the faces of friends, the anxieties, joys, and challenges I faced as a young man. When I look down at the scuffed earth beneath that swing, I'm reminded too of the generations of students, before and since, who have passed that way and found that place as important to their life stories as I did.

We celebrate today the Feast of the Most Holy Trinity, the most distinctive doctrine in the Church's treasury of truth. Doctrines, unfortunately, suffer from some bad press in our world. Too often they are regarded as flat, informational entries consigned to books and left to experts, abstract mathematical formulas worked out by others but of little interest to most of us in the real world. Doctrines, however, are meant to be the memory-carriers of our faith tradition, like the swing at my alma mater. They evoke the stories of faith that tell us who we are and how we got here, reminding us that other feet have passed this way and many people have found this place important to their life stories.

The doctrine of the Trinity contains a summary of the entire narrative of the ways we have come to understand and experience God over millennia. It is like a zip file—for those of you who are somewhat computer literate—a compressed, easily transmittable package of important information. Which is to say, it has to be unzipped by the user. If it is not unzipped, it may look pretty, but it doesn't do anything. But if it is unzipped, it unfolds in a myriad of ways, conducting us into a four-dimensional world of experience we might otherwise miss.

"It's a great mystery," we say. "It's a great mystery." The Trinity certainly is that. But mystery, too, suffers from some misunderstanding. Too often, to call something a mystery is to say it's unfathomable, like facing a wall of darkness into which we dare not venture. The doctrine of the Trinity celebrates precisely that God has lit that darkness with God's own self-revelation, and that God beckons us into loving relationship with the very heart and mind of God. Far from being inscrutable, the Judeo-Christian sense of mystery is infinitely intelligible. We direct our our deepest life longings to it. So rather than throw up our hands in resignation before it, the doctrine of the Trinity reminds us that we are all called to be seekers, people called to the journey of heart, mind, and will, the restless adventure of spirit, which is faith.

It's amazing, really, how practical today's feast might be for us if we open it up. Not only does it remind us of a rich fund of memories; it reminds us that we are on a voyage of discovery that will carry us through and beyond this life. Not only does it reassure us that God is not some distant, impersonal force dwelling in splendid isolation, aloof from the world where we live, but it affirms a God who is personal through and through, enmeshed in the created world, always working for our good, infusing us with life and energy—a God whose very being is both unity and community.

Not only does this feast tell us who God is; it also tells us who we are, and the potential of what we can yet become. We too can be creators. We too can enter relationships deeply. We too can be builders of community. We too can be liberators of the poor and oppressed. We too can serve, suffer with, and empower.

As St. Paul reminds us, we are nothing less than children of God; that is to say, heirs, adult offspring who share fully in the life of the family, destined for glory.

Commentary

There are few homiletic challenges greater than preaching on the Feast of the Holy Trinity. Catechists, similarly, find this central doctrine of the Christian faith difficult to convey in a way that is lucid and meaningful without being too abstract. Approached in our too often über-rational way, a use of reason that is too narrow, it is difficult to bend our minds around a concept of God as one in three. Some preachers and teachers attempt to wrestle with the meaning of *person* in the Godhead, or even launch into speculative theology about the interpersonal dynamics within God. Ordinary folks quickly get lost in terrain that even the brightest theologians find tremendously challenging to think through and articulate coherently.

Part of the problem is that we forget the meaning and purpose of doctrines. Doctrines are meant to express succinctly truths and experiences to which we are meant to hand ourselves over through contemplation. In other words, doctrines are meant to be unfolded and prayed, both privately and corporately. They are not illogical nor unreasonable, but supra-rational, containing a logic that may be of a relational or mystical type, not empirically verifiable. Moreover, we need to keep doctrines linked to the biblical narratives from which they spring. It is not wise — and really, not even possible — to explain what the doctrine of the Trinity or any doctrine means without resort to salvation history as revealed in the Bible. The doctrine of the Trinity attempts to span and sum up, in the most adequate (or least inadequate!) human words, what God's people have learned about the divine partner in a relationship of crucial importance over many centuries.

This particular preaching effort avoids the kind of abstract speculation that has little homiletic payoff. It celebrates the doctrine as a pinnacle achievement, but one that invites further exploration with both mind and heart. It approaches the Trinity as an inviting mystery, a visible reminder that all of us are invited into a lifetime of dynamic relationship with a good God who has freely chosen to reveal God's own self, but who remains beyond our ability to fully fathom. Moreover, the homily reminds us that the doctrine rests upon several legs grounded in the narratives of the Scriptures and makes no sense cut off from those stories of faith. The vein of this homily could be thought of as a kind of wisdom theology, a theological tradition not well enough appreciated by contemporary Christians, heirs as we are to an Enlightenment-scientific tradition of isolating and defining things. The biblical wisdom tradition, by way of contrast, and the tradition of Christian theology as wisdom ground practical advice for living the faith in the world. In this case, the doctrine of the Most Holy Trinity summarizes God as one who creates, reveals, forms a people, promises blessing, comes to save, suffers with. The hearer is invited into that God, and even to become like that God by doing the same sorts of things. Thus the mystery pointed to by the doctrine is rendered participative, one might even say, "user friendly." This should be of assistance to catechumens in their process of initial introduction to the faith. However, it may well also be helpful to baptized Christians who have long since given up trying to understand the meaning of this doctrine and this liturgical feast.

Homily 2 • Mass of Christmas Eve
Isaiah 9:1–6 • Titus 2:11–14 • Luke 2:1–14 • Michael E. Connors, csc

Wasn't there an easier way than this? I mean, for God to save the world, couldn't there have been a simpler way to do it? A divine snap of the fingers, for instance. An edict from on high. A display of convincing power in the sky, something that over-awes the inhabitants of earth, sending our enemies scurrying for cover. No way would I have sent my own son—nuh-uh, not without a phalanx of bodyguards, an army and navy so immense as to make any resistance foolish. What did he think would happen? Of course we killed him. That's what we do. The violence without is a symptom of the disorder and desperation within. And if I had anything to say about it, he would have come as a full-grown adult, complete with a palace, multiple servants, a hot shower and a good haircut, royal purple and gold and, most of all, no question about who is boss.

Instead, we get a filthy, stinking stable behind a crowded inn. We get unlikely first-time parents, no-account people being numbered by a great empire for tax purposes, vulnerable, far from home. We get barn animals, oinking and squawking, neighing and mooing, bellowing and bleating, and doing those things animals do. . . . We get uneducated, unwashed shepherds as the first visitors. And we get an utterly helpless human infant, laid in a grain box, squalling in the night. Such a messy, smelly, improbable story.

Did it have to be this way? Evidently, God's imagination is stranger than mine.

It is dark here, isn't it? — just as Isaiah said, "a people who walk in darkness." Take a good look around. Lots of strife, terror, poverty, sickness, premature death. Global warming. ISIS butchery. Institutions that betray us or just don't work. The darkness even fingers its way into our own hearts and homes. But instead of the "great light" the prophet promised, we get . . . a slim candle in the nighttime. Attractive, yes, even mesmerizing. But it looks like it could be extinguished with a single puff. As fragile as a child's breath. Where is the might and glory?

Could it be that God's imagination is bigger than ours?

Really, I hate messes — especially when they are of my own making. Sometimes the mess we've made of the world gets under my skin, too. And not a week goes by that I don't feel like I'm stuck cleaning up somebody else's thoughtlessness of others, somebody's failure to follow through, somebody's disrespect for others or things or our planet. I want things to be perfect, or at least something approaching what they can be. I certainly want the Son of God, the Savior of humankind, to get better treatment.

Then I notice that he is born into the middle of a mess. Not just a messy, smelly place unfit for human habitation, not just the bloody mess of childbirth, but into the middle of a world of gross injustice, greed, and misused power, a world that will shortly send him and his parents fleeing across borders as refugees.

God's imagination must be way bigger than ours. God must truly have an amazing love affair with human flesh and human possibility to come not as a ruler, not at the head of a conquering army laying down the law, not as a freshly scrubbed prince whose life is otherworldly and shielded from our sight, but as one of us, a baby. A baby born mostly unnoticed to poor parents in a small town, growing into the same sadnesses and joys, tragedies and moments of light we are given. God must love messes. If he would willingly be born into such a mess, there is no mess you or I can make that he would shrink from. If God loves the mess of humanity so much, who are we to disdain it? God comes to find us in our messes.

God's imagination is bigger than ours. Yet God's imagination for human life is not only beyond us, but also *in* us. In the midst of the darkness, in the midst of the rotting messes all around us, will we dream with God?

Commentary

What is at stake in Christmas preaching is, of course, the doctrine of the incarnation. What is at stake in the incarnation? Everything Catholic Christians believe:

- an understanding of God and how God works with human beings
- the sacraments
- the working of grace, a sharing in God's own life.
- the doctrine of the redemption itself

The challenge of preaching at Christmas, both for catechumens and for the baptized, is to get beyond some of the cultural accretions that cloud its meaning and help people see why it matters, why it is more than a sentimental story. Even mostly uncatechized catechumens bring with them some notions of what Christmas is, and while these may not be wrong, they are likely to be quite incomplete.

This homily attempts to invite the hearer into a fresh and thoughtful (re-)appreciation of the Christmas story. So much of the Gospel story, especially from Matthew and Luke, is so very unlikely, even shocking. Yet in the hearer's mind, some layers of sweet sentimentality may have to be peeled back before the story jolts us the way it should. The homily brings to the fore of the imagination the difficulty and messiness of the scene, as well as the brokenness of the general human situation. Where we are tempted to overlook or even disdain the human condition, God embraces it and immerses God's very self into it. As St. Gregory of Nazianzus famously said, "That which is not assumed [in the incarnation] is not redeemed."[10] Christmas is God's dream for a better humanity and a better world. Precisely therein lies its powerful message of hope for us.

---

10. Gregory of Nazianzus "Critique of Apollinarius and Apollinarianism," Epistle 101.

Chapter 6

The Rites of Sending and Election

My brothers and sisters, in beginning this period of Lent, we look forward to celebrating at Easter the life-giving mysteries of our Lord's suffering, death, and resurrection. These elect, whom we bring with us to the Easter sacraments, will look to us for an example of Christian renewal. Let us pray to the Lord for them and for ourselves, that we may be renewed by one another's efforts and together come to share the joys of Easter.

RCIA, 134

On the Sunday morning of the Rite of Sending, it always seemed to me that there was a special electricity in the air as the parish community gathered. Lent itself is such a specially graced time in parish life, a time of special attention to discipleship and what it asks of all of us. For initiating parishes, the presence of catechumens standing publicly before us again, to take their next step in the journey, lends a special kind of weight and urgency to the liturgical season. Those to be elected by the bishop that same afternoon would arrive at the parish church in the morning, their faces already beaming with a kind of earnest but happy anticipation of what lay ahead. They knew they were about to profess publicly the importance of their faith, a public confession of faith that would be reaffirmed in Baptism just six weeks hence at Easter. They had come far, over many months, and they were nearing their goal. So for all of us Lent's serious, even somber self-examination and asceticism were tinged with the joy of accompanying others falling in step with us on the road that leads to Calvary and Easter. There is serious business at hand for the catechumens and for all of us, for the work of identifying and uprooting sin is a time of personal vulnerability and change. But that work is sustained by the hope that we walk with the Savior, who confronted the forces of sin and death and overcame them.

The Rite of Sending for Election and the Rite of Election ordinarily occur on the same day, and ordinarily that day is the First Sunday of Lent. They are best approached as two movements of one whole, forming together the second major step in the process, the passageway into the final period of preparation for the Easter sacraments. These rites are preceded by a process of discernment, which determines that certain of the catechumens have advanced far enough in their personal growth and in their understanding and living of the Christian way that they are deemed ready for the celebration of Baptism, Confirmation, and Eucharist at the upcoming Easter Vigil celebration. The *Rite of Christian Initiation of Adults* describes the required the readiness this way:

> Before the rite of election is celebrated, the catechumens are expected to have undergone a conversion in mind and in action and to have developed a sufficient acquaintance with Christian teaching as well as a spirit of faith and charity. With deliberate will and an enlightened faith they must have the intention to receive the sacraments of the Church, a resolve they will express publicly in the actual celebration of the rite. (RCIA, 120)

This process of discernment is shared by the catechumens, their catechetical team, and their sponsors and godparents, and should not be taken lightly. Indeed, the RCIA charges all concerned with the catechumens' formation to "consider the matter carefully" (RCIA, 121; see also 122).

Since the catechumenate is to be a substantial period, and one with a formidable catechetical agenda, it is to be expected that catechumens will need at least one liturgical year at this stage, depending upon the assessment of their personal needs. The result can often be that some catechumens are deemed ready for the coming Easter, while others are not. By its very nature as a celebration of the foundation of Christian faith and the new life it offers, Easter is the ideal and strongly preferred time for the culmination of the initiation process. However, when necessary, the sacraments of initiation can be celebrated at other times during the year, as well.

The Rite of Sending of the Catechumens for Election

The Rite of Sending is optional yet pastorally should never be omitted unless the Rite of Election takes place in the same church. It is essentially a nomination ceremony, a liturgical celebration of a parish community's discernment that these particular candidates are ready to go forward for the Easter sacraments about seven weeks hence. This readiness is a conclusion reached at the local level, while the final decision, or "election" for the sacraments, belongs to the local bishop. As the *Rite of Christian Initiation of Adults* acknowledges, "It is within the parish community that the preliminary judgment is made concerning the catechumens' state of formation and progress." The text continues with an explanation of the Rite of Sending: "This rite offers that local community the opportunity to express its approval of the catechumens and to send them forth to the celebration of election assured of the parish's care and support" (RCIA, 107).

The Rite of Sending may take place in a separate celebration of the Word, but is best celebrated after the homily at a parish Sunday Mass, at which the candidates' catechists, sponsors, godparents, family members, and a good crowd of parishioners are present. It is a simple but highly meaningful ritual. The director of the catechumenate presents the candidates publicly and calls each forward by name. The presiding minister then makes formal inquiry from the catechumens' godparents as to the readiness of the candidates. The presiding minister asks three questions of the godparents:

> Have these catechumens taken their formation in the Gospel and in the Catholic way of life seriously?
>
> Have they given evidence of their conversion by the example of their lives?
>
> Do you judge them to be ready to be presented to the bishop for the rite of election? (RCIA, 112)

At this point, some parish communities also afford the godparent the opportunity to say a few additional words of endorsement for their candidates by way of describing the person's progress in faith and growth in charity and other virtues. Such testimony can be highly personal and moving for the whole assembly. The celebrant may then also invite the whole assembly to express its approval by a round of applause. After this, the minister affirms the recommendation of the candidates for election, concluding, "May God bring to completion the good work he has begun in you" (RCIA, 112). The presider then invites the candidates to sign the Book of the Elect, unless the signing is to be done later at the Rite of Election.

The liturgical assembly then prays for the catechumens through special prayers of intercession. The presider introduces the intercessions through these or similar words:

> My brothers and sisters, we look forward to celebrating at Easter the life-giving mysteries of our Lord's suffering, death and resurrection. As we journey together to the Easter sacraments, these catechumens will look to us for an example of Christian renewal. Let us pray to the Lord for them and for ourselves, that we may be renewed by one another's efforts and together come to share the joys of Easter. (RCIA, 114)

The presider then closes the intercessions with a special, solemn prayer over the catechumens. He then dismisses the catechumens as usual, making special reference to their being sent to the bishop.

The Rite of Election or Enrollment of Names

The Rite of Election ordinarily takes place in the cathedral and is presided over by the bishop. If the bishop is unable to attend, he may specially delegate another priest to preside. Normally the Rite takes place near the beginning of Lent, most often the afternoon of the First Sunday of Lent. This rite closes the period of the catechumenate and begins "the period of final, more intense preparation for the sacraments of initiation, during which the elect will be encouraged to follow Christ with greater generosity" (RCIA, 118). The text of the RCIA explains that this rite constitutes a ratification, not only of the discernment done at the parish level but, more profoundly, of the movement and call of God. Thus the rite expresses a mutual commitment between the Church and the candidates:

> This step is called election because the acceptance made by the Church is founded on the election of God, in whose name the Church acts. The step is also called the enrollment of names because as a pledge of fidelity the

candidates inscribe their names in the book that lists those who have been chosen for initiation. (RCIA, 119)

Thus, the Church acts based on what God has been doing with these candidates. At the same time, the Church elicits a deeper level of commitment and faithfulness from the candidates. From this point forward until Baptism, these catechumens are called "the elect."

The Rite of Election takes place in the context of either a Mass or a celebration of the Word. After the readings, the bishop gives a homily, which "should address not just the catechumens but the entire community of the faithful, so that all will be encouraged to give good example and to accompany the elect along the path of the paschal mystery" (RCIA, 129). Then the bishop calls the catechumens forward by name with their godparents. If the number of candidates is so great as to preclude the possibility of calling each by name, the RCIA advises the parish catechists that there should be "a special celebration beforehand in which they call each candidate forward by name" (RCIA, 130). This would seem to be the optional Rite of Sending to be celebrated in the parish. The bishop then elicits the testimony of the godparents or sponsors and, optionally, the approval of the whole assembly. The Rite offers two forms for this. In the first, the bishop poses a single question to the godparents: "As God is your witness, do you consider these candidates worthy to be admitted to the sacraments of Christian initiation?" (RCIA, 131.A) In the second form, the bishop askes three questions:

Have [the candidates] faithfully listened to God's word proclaimed by the Church?

Have they responded to that word and begun to walk in God's presence?

Have they shared the company of their Christian brothers and sisters and joined with them in prayer? (RCIA, 131.B)

In response, the bishop then asks the candidates to affirm publicly their desire for this step. This desire is solemnized by the enrollment of their names in the Book of the Elect. Then the bishop formally calls the candidates to the sacraments at the upcoming Easter and pronounces them members of the elect. A series of intercessions for the candidates' continued growth and progress follows. After the intercessions, the bishop, with hands stretched out in blessing, prays a special prayer over the elect. Finally, if the rite is taking place in the context of Mass, the bishop or presider dismisses the elect. If the Eucharist is not celebrated, the presider dismisses the entire assembly.

Preaching the Rites of Sending and Election

The Rites of Sending and Election have parallel structures, and their rich homiletic possibilities are intertwined. The homily takes place before the Rite of Sending. Here is a brief examination of some of those possibilities.

Proclamation of Christian Identity

The calling and enrollment of names is a strikingly personal element to these rites. Each candidate for election is named publicly. As at the Rite of Acceptance, the public nature of this event is not incidental; it represents a commitment and proclamation of Christian identity. In some ages of Christian history and in some places even today such a public step could put a person in danger of persecution. This could be an occasion to talk about the suffering and even martyrdom that perennially mark the witness of Christians in the world.

Biblical Connections to Calling by Name

Moreover, being called by name has deep biblical resonances. There are numerous instances of call narratives in the Scriptures, and in nearly all of these the uttering of the person's name figures prominently. Modern hearers will need some assistance in understanding what was at stake in the ancient world in giving, receiving, or uttering a person's name. There is a connotation of intimacy and ongoing relationship. Similarly, one of the high points of the Hebrew Bible is Exodus 3:14, the disclosure of the divine name. Here the signal is that God wishes to be known to the people, personally, and in a way that guarantees both Moses' authority and the Lord's promise of deliverance from the Egyptians.

The candidates, similarly, have been called by name—by God, most importantly. God has called them close to God's own Self, summoned them uniquely and irrevocably into relationship with God, thereby ratifying the personal worth of each person. The Church dares to speak the name of each candidate because God has first done so. The Church affirms and rejoices in what God is accomplishing within each person, and thus welcomes each into a new stage of accompaniment on the journey. The homilist can and should broaden this sense of call to all those within hearing distance of the homily, for all are distinctively and personally called. This is the meaning of election, God's choice of a people uniquely God's own. "Thus says the Lord, who created you, Jacob, and formed you, Israel: Do not fear, for I have redeemed you; I have called you by name: you are mine" (Isaiah 43:1, NRSV). The bishop expresses the Church's call to the sacraments based on God's call at work in the candidates' lives. As the candidates inscribe their signatures, so all of us are called to respond with a commitment of our whole selves, which is exactly what the name signified in the ancient context.

Testimony of Godparents and Sponsors

The testimony of the godparents can be another homiletic point of departure. The very existence of these roles and their public nature suggest a homily on the importance of mentorship in the Christian life. This message might help to lift up the entire community to their own need for guidance and to their shared obligation to train the young and guide newcomers into the fullness of the Christian way. In God's graciousness, he appoints shepherds to guide his people, and while this role falls most especially to the clergy, it finds echoes in other mentoring roles in the community, too.

The nature of the personal testimony sought from the godparents is also instructive. Each of the questions asked of the godparents or at the Rite of Sending and the Rite of Election points to an important aspect of discipleship. "Have these catechumens taken their formation in the Gospel and in the Catholic way of life seriously?" (RCIA, 112). Quite often, in actual practice, the visibility of catechumens seriously about the business of learning and growing in the faith encourages the already baptized to take their own spiritual growth more seriously and pursue it more intentionally. The homilist can accent this and raise it to consciousness for the whole community. The catechumens have already honored us with their desire to join our ranks. Now their zeal should encourage the entire community to renew theirs.

Listening to the Scriptural Texts

"Have they faithfully listened to God's word proclaimed by the Church?" (RCIA, 131.B). This question presents an excellent opportunity for the preacher to help the whole assembly to appreciate just how vitally necessary for all of us is deep listening to the scriptural texts, especially the Sunday Lectionary selections. As St. Paul says, "faith comes from what is heard, and what is heard comes through the word of Christ" (Romans 10:17). The Word of God is the staple of catechumenal formation. For all of us, there is no progress in the Christian spiritual life without a serious confrontation with the Bible.

"Have they given evidence of their conversion by the example of their lives?" (RCIA, 112). "Have they responded to that word and begun to walk in God's presence?" (RCIA, 131.B). These questions point to the connections between word and deed, faith and practice in everyday life. They remind one of the old saying, "If you were put on trial for being a Christian, would there be enough evidence to convict you?" The homilist can help to emphasize that faith comes to full flower in the way we live our lives. Hearing the Word of God leads one into deeper relationship with God, and that relationship matures in the works of charity lived in everyday life.

"Have they shared the company of their Christian brothers and sisters and joined with them in prayer?" (RCIA, 131.B). This question presents the homilist with an avenue for challenging all of his hearers to grasp, or be reminded of, the role of *koinonia* (community) and *leitourgia* (worship) in our journey with the Lord. The Christian walk is never isolated. It presumes the support and companionship of others. Moreover, its focus is always on the presence of the living Lord.

The Bishop: Symbol of the Wider Church

The bishop is an important symbolic presence in this passage of the catechumens into final preparation, and one could say that he is one of the liturgical "texts" that can inform the homily at either the Rite of Sending or the Rite of Election. The homilist may want to use this occasion to explore some of the various aspects of the meaning of the episcopal office. For example, the bishop is a successor to the Apostles, so one could speak about the unbroken transmission of the apostolic mandate, "Go into all the world and proclaim the good news to the whole creation" (Mark 16:15, NRSV). We who share the Good News and evangelize do so in union with the worldwide college of bishops, and through them, with all of our brothers and sisters in the faith. Likewise, the bishop represents the paradoxical Catholic understanding of church as both local and universal. He presides over the local diocese, but in his union with bishops the world over, he also represents our union with Christians elsewhere and down through the centuries. Candidates who attend the Rite of Election along with candidates from parishes throughout the diocese often report that it is impressive and illuminating for them to see and meet catechumens from other places. The rite conveys a vivid sense of the wider church, the Body of Christ in the world.

Within all of the themes mentioned so far, the homilist might do well to call upon the exhortation the celebrant gives to the assembly at the beginning of the intercessions for the catechumens: "These catechumens will look to us for an example of Christian renewal. Let us pray to the Lord for them and for ourselves, that we may be renewed by one another's efforts and together come to share the joys of Easter" (RCIA, 114). These statements offer an outstanding opportunity for the preacher to emphasize the relationship between the candidates and the whole parish community. Our paths join together in mutual support. While the catechumens look to the wider community for witness and example, the community draws strength from the dedication and spiritual thirst of the catechumens. These connections are not merely theoretical; people from the catechumens and the parish community frequently report that they have been inspired and renewed in faith through joining in this process.

Scripture Readings of the Day

Finally, the Scripture readings of the day are, of course, an important source for the homilist. In all three liturgical cycles, the Gospel reading is one of the synoptic versions of Jesus going out to the desert and being tempted by the devil (Cycle A: Matthew 4:1–11; Cycle B: Mark 1:12–15; Cycle C: Luke 4:1–13). These Gospel texts are powerful segues into the meaning and purpose of Lent. With Jesus, the elect go on retreat in the desert, so to speak. As Jesus was preparing for his public ministry, so the elect want to be ready for the public celebration of the central mysteries of the faith in Holy Thursday, Good Friday, and Easter, and to be ready for their Baptism in the light of the Easter event. Naturally, the rest of the community joins in as a season for its own renewal, walking toward the celebration of the Paschal Mystery and reaffirmation of its baptismal promises.

The narratives of Jesus in the desert offer the preacher several possibilities. Note that Jesus' sojourn in the desert has a purpose, but that purpose is not some kind of self-inflicted punishment. While the desert can be harsh, more importantly it is a place of great clarity and singularity. Shorn of our usual concerns and encumbrances, the bright light of the desert helps us see ourselves and see God more clearly. The desert can heighten our awareness of what really matters and of what we really need to survive.

Nevertheless, the starkness of the desert landscape can tempt us to various kinds of escapism. Our desire is not to avoid temptation but to meet and overcome it. Jesus' temptations are traditionally understood as the standard human temptations to wealth, prestige, and power. The homilist can concretize our purpose to resist temptation through explanation of the traditional disciplines of Lent: prayer, fasting, and almsgiving or service. These practices hone the spiritual senses so that the participant is prepared to be fully alert to the powerfully transformative celebrations of the Triduum. The traditional triad of ascetic disciplines of Lent, and our direct confrontation with temptation, serve to purify us of illusions, false gods, and misdirected desires.

The homilist will find numerous possible bridges between these sacred texts and the various parts of the Rites of Sending and Election. God's choice invites our response, our ever fuller and deeper conversion, and promises us a share in His life, which regenerates and heals us.

Homily ▪ Rite of Sending ▪ 1st Sunday of Lent, Cycle C
Deuteronomy 26:4–10 ▪ Romans 10:8–13 ▪ Luke 4:1–13
Michael E. Connors, CSC

Over the years I have taken groups of students to the desert in the Southwest US — one year to Arizona and Sonora, another year to El

Paso, Texas, and Juarez, Mexico. These were not vacations, nor service trips, but brief educational immersion trips to our southern border region. The purpose was to meet people and hear their stories, especially the stories of people who have crossed that line in the sand, or climbed the wall we've built, in order to better understand the pastoral, legal, and economic issues surrounding migration. It's always an education for me too, for these are places of social and cultural realities quite different from what most of us are used to, and I think they have a lot to teach us. The most humbling thing is to encounter God in the faith of people who face so many daily difficulties and have risked so much trying to find a better life.

As a native Midwesterner, I'm always struck by a couple of things about the desert environment that seem radically different from my experience. One is that the air is different: it's dry and crystal clear. Another is that because the air is different and there is little humidity, the light is different too. The sun shines nearly all the time, and it shines with an intensity that makes for rich contrasts. The shadows are deep and razor-sharp. The bright light and lack of vegetation mean that everything seems exposed: there are few places to hide. The sun exposes variations of color, contour, and texture one could easily miss in the grayer, hazier light of Indiana. I used to think the desert was a harsh, ugly, and hostile environment to be avoided. Today I understand that the desert is a place of incredible visual clarity — challenging in its own way, to be sure, but also immensely beautiful for those who welcome its challenges and are prepared for its demands.

The season of Lent is a sort of voluntary sojourn in the desert. We willingly submit ourselves to the scrutiny of its bright light, which comes to us through the challenge of the Scripture readings and through our Lenten disciplines of fasting, prayer, and almsgiving or service of others. Lent is meant to be a place of visual clarity, clarity about God and clarity about ourselves. Lived well, it exposes to us our rough edges and imperfections, leaving us no place to hide the truth from ourselves. More importantly, it exposes to us the truth that, in the end, we really do have only God, and the truth that this God loves us so intensely, so unselfishly that he would willingly lay down his life for us to reach our full potential. We go to the desert to proclaim with Moses and the people that we too are the children of refugees, illegal aliens who cried out to God in our misery and oppression, and were heard and saved by nothing less than the "strong hand and outstretched arms" of our Savior. In the strong light of Lent there is awesome beauty.

In a special way we go into the desert with these catechumens, whom today we will call by name and send to the bishop with the request that they be chosen for Baptism at Easter. Their godparents will give testimony to God's work in their lives, the choice God has already made to draw them to himself. These men and women have faithfully listened with us to the Word of God and joined with us on the way of following Christ. This afternoon, they will join with other catechumens from across our diocese, and through the bishop, in union with others throughout the world. For them, and for us, this Lent will be a special season of purification, a time of earnest final preparation.

Jesus has gone before us into the desert. Before beginning his public ministry, he went to the wilderness for his Lent. Note that Luke says not that Jesus wandered into the desert by accident, but that the Spirit *led* or *drove* Jesus into the desert for forty days where he faced the tempter. The face of evil he confronted there, the temptations that met him there, are not unique to the desert. These are temptations that assail us always and everywhere. They are easier to identify and resist in the clarity of the noonday desert sun. But this is only, as it were, to give us the practice we need so that we can recognize them in the fuzzier, cloudier places we usually inhabit.

Indeed, we should get to know these temptations very well, for in one form or another they already know us well. There is the temptation to over-reliance on the things of this earth. We can easily spend much of life looking for the next creature comfort, the next pleasure, the security we think we need, or protecting and hoarding those we already have.

There is the temptation to fame. Even those of us who shun the limelight want to be well thought of, so we chameleon-*ize* ourselves, shape ourselves to what we think others want, and try to impress.

There is also the temptation to power. So much within and around us sends the message that meaning and self-worth depend upon how many people we dominate, how much money we make, how many programs and projects we manage.

These are traps into which all of us fall at one time or another. They distract us from God, and they stunt our growth as people. Today we celebrate that Jesus himself met them and prevailed over them, and it's fortunate for us that he did. Now he wants to help us overcome them as well, that we might be as free as he was to offer his life's energies to God and others.

These temptations will meet us this week, and next, inviting us to cut corners, make little compromises, and put ourselves first. But God will be there to meet us too. His light is bright enough to keep us from harm and show us the way. And he is leading his band of immigrants through the desert to a land flowing with milk and honey.

Commentary

On the First Sunday of Lent a presider and preacher can often feel like a lot is going on. The catechumens, or at least some of them, are moving toward the culmination of their training in faith. Their readiness has been discerned prayerfully, and now they are dispatched to the bishop for what is likely their first experience of church larger than their home parish. Meanwhile, the whole parish enters the Lenten season, a season typically marked in parish life by a multiplication of activities and quickening pace. The day is full of homiletic opportunity for all.

This particular homily may try to do too much at the possible expense of that clear unity that helps to make a preacher's words "stick" in the minds and hearts of the hearers throughout the coming week. The unifying image here, of course, is the desert. Most people today do not have a direct experience of the desert upon which to draw visually. Moreover, Lent has often been presented as a season of harshness and difficulty, rather than as a season of "joy," as one of the Lenten Prefaces describes it. So the homilist should not presume that the assembly, either the catechumens or the baptized, really understands positively what the invitation of Lent presents to us. The point of a retreat in the desert is not the harshness but the clarity of vision and the laying aside of everything else to spend time with God and God alone. Lent is not a fearful, burdensome season, but a time of ever-greater freedom and sharpening of spiritual insight as we process toward Easter's bright glory.

This homily attempts to ground the season in God's goodness, affording us clarity of insight and a season of renewal and mercy. God's lavish generosity comes to each of us by name. We are called and chosen.

As the catechumens are now called and chosen to stand among the elect, so they remind us of God's having dared to utter our names and summon us into union with him. In a real sense, the elect will lead us through the exercises and disciplines of Lent. Together the Lord sustains us by the promise that we can and must rely solely on God for all we need. A transformed life, a life of joy provided by God's love, awaits us and begins even now.

At the same time, and based on God's gracious choice of us as God's People, the homily also offers the deep challenge of self-examination. Temptation is a fact of human life, but as disciples, we can get wiser about what it means and in what kinds of illusions it is typically masked. Again, the goal is freedom, deeper discipleship, the rooting of God's own generosity within us. Our companion and guide is none other than Christ himself, who met the same sorts of temptations we face. With him, we too can overcome those temptations and allow him to purify our desires.

Note, finally, that this homily is preached to the whole assembly, not simply to those being sent and elected for the Easter sacraments. While it could be possible to construct a homily for this occasion that speaks directly and exclusively to the catechumens, and thus speaks to the rest of the assembly as an "overhearing," such a strategy seems somewhat artificial and risks losing the attention of the already initiated. The central focus of preaching is always on God, what God is doing, has done, and wants to do. All of us need to hear this because all of us participate in it. While the catechumens are in a special role among us, the preacher should resist the temptation to over-personalize the liturgical occasion or lionize the catechumens for what they are doing. They are, like the rest of us, redeemed sinners. And the Lenten journey is all about the road to redemption in Christ Jesus.

Chosen for the Easter sacraments, the elect now embark upon their period of final preparation for full initiation, a spiritual retreat, as it were, through the season of Lent.

Chapter 7

Purification and Enlightenment

A clean heart create for me, God; renew in me a steadfast spirit.

Psalm 51:12

From Election to Easter

Commentator Jan Michael Joncas tells us that the Period of Purification and Enlightenment is "the most densely structured of all the stages of initiation,"[1] and that is certainly true. It is also the shortest stage, a mere six weeks, normally coinciding with Lent. During this period, the intensity builds in anticipation of the celebration of Easter, at which the elect will be baptized and confirmed and share the Eucharist for the first time.

The *Rite of Christian Initiation of Adults* describes this period as "a time for spiritual recollection in preparation for the celebration of the paschal mystery" (RCIA 138), and "a period of more intense spiritual preparation, consisting more in interior reflection than in catechetical instruction" (RCIA, 139). The clear intent here is that catechesis, as instruction in the major tenets of the faith, is already complete before the celebration of the Rite of Election. The Period of Purification and Enlightenment is not a time for introducing new material to the elect. It is, rather, a time of going deeper into what has already been presented, and, more importantly, allowing those truths to go deeper into the personalities of the elect, so that they may be spiritually prepared for the celebrations of the Triduum, amidst which their full initiation into the Church will be celebrated. This does not mean, of course, that the catechesis that the catechumens have internalized is devoid of

---

1. Jan Michael Joncas, *Preaching the Rites of Initiation* (Chicago: Liturgy Training Publications, 1994), 39.

95

spirituality or not infused with prayer; that would be inherently contrary to the spirit and nature of the catechetical development of the catechumens, or of anyone else, for that matter. During this period, however, the balance and flavor shift to a more spiritual, interior, and prayerful reflection—in other words, a difference of degree and intensity rather than of kind. As the Rite continues, the hope of this period is "to purify the minds and hearts of the elect as they search their own consciences and do penance . . . [and] to enlighten the minds and hearts of the elect with a deeper knowledge of Christ the Savior" (RCIA, 139). The Period of Purification and Enlightenment, then, is more like a pre-initiation retreat for the elect, and the rest of the Church joins in this retreat for its own renewal in faith.

The period presents the homilist with at least six unique preaching opportunities: three scrutinies, two presentations, plus the preparatory rites of Holy Saturday. To those we will turn shortly, but a few general observations about preaching during Lent are in order.

We know that Lent is the Church's one penitential season, both for the elect and for the baptized. However, the preacher should have a clear understanding of what Christian penitence is, and what it is not. *Penitence* refers to an attitude springing from a humble but honest recognition of one's failures and character limitations, and is marked by contrition for one's sins. The season invites *repentance* and *conversion*, etymologically a "turning around" or "turning back," connoting a resolve to change one's behavior or orientation. The *penance* to be undertaken in the season is thus not to be construed as a punishment for sin, much less a pretext for self-hatred or self-abuse, for, arguably, we can never bear the punishment or repair the damage which strict justice might require for our misdeeds. The point is to look honestly at our lives, feel sorrow for what we have done wrong, make amends to the extent we can, and commit to change.

The etymology of the word *Lent* is also instructive for us. *Lent* comes from a Middle English word for springtime; the root is the same as in our word *lengthen*, a reference to the lengthening of the daylight hours in the spring of the Northern Hemisphere. Lent, in other words, is the Church's springtime, a season of refreshment, renewal, and blossoming new life out of the apparent death of winter. This means that the season has a joyful, hopeful quality to it. Release from sin is a birth to freedom! Repentance is still possible! Mercy is promised! Indeed the Lenten Preface I refers to Lent as a season marked by "the joy of minds made pure." The preacher will want to stress that the honest self-examination called for in Lent is really a joy-filled opportunity to unburden ourselves from the constrictions of self-preoccupation and thoughtlessness of others or of God. The goal and promise of Lent is new or renewed freedom to be who we are, our truest and best created selves. Too often, Lent has been presented to Catholics as a season of self-deprecation to be endured with a stiff upper lip, a season of wallowing in guilt and shame, when in fact its purpose should be to sharpen the spiritual senses and turn the mind and heart toward the joy to be found in God's life within us.

Of course, to accomplish its goals in us, Lent does entail certain disciplines. These *disciplines* are related to *discipleship*, a key Lenten theme which invites us to more closely follow and imitate the person of Christ, especially in his willingness to suffer for love of us and love of the Father. The Lenten Lectionary readings build in intensity as we follow Christ ever more closely to his betrayal, condemnation, brutal death, and ultimate triumph over death. The readings can build in us a greater confidence that there are loves and truths marking our lives that are worth suffering for, and a greater confidence that death will not have the last word. The magnitude and profundity of this message is such that Lenten preachers need to help us prepare to take this message in, to see its life-giving relevance for all areas of our lives, put our faith in it and willingly enact this narrative in our own life stories.

The Sunday Lectionary readings in all three cycles begin with Jesus himself going out to the desert or wilderness for a time of intense communion with the Father. Though sinless, Christ undertakes a Lent in the desert, a place of great clarity and solitude. Here Jesus meets the Tempter and stands firm against the temptations to devote his life to material comfort, prestige, and power—temptations that assail all of us in one form or another. He shows us how to triumph over them and devote our lives entirely to God. This day, the First Sunday of Lent, is the normal time for celebrating the Rites of Sending and Election.

On the Second Sunday of Lent Jesus and his closest friends go up to the mountaintop, where he is transfigured before their eyes. His unique identity is revealed before us, and the Gospel challenges us to put our faith in him. However, his transfiguration also foreshadows what is possible for us as we submit to the power of the divine life. We too can be transformed into a divinized version of ourselves, far beyond anything we can do for ourselves.

The final Sunday of Lent, Palm or Passion Sunday, launches us into the narrative that dominates Holy Week: Jesus' triumphal entry into Jerusalem, leading to the first of two annual readings of versions of the Passion. This is where the whole season has been leading, the climax of the story. Do we dare follow him here? It is easy to shout "Hosanna!" but more difficult to stand beneath the Cross. The liturgies call us to walk with him, step by painful step. As we do, we may discover anew that he walks with us as well, especially in the sorrows we bear and the sufferings we endure.

A subtheme of the season in all cycles has to do with water, the very antithesis of the desert where we began our journey. We are moving toward the life-giving waters of Baptism at the Easter Vigil, the elect for the first time, the rest of us as an opportunity for reminder, renewal and recommitment. Even water is a multivalent symbol in the Christian faith. It cleanses, slakes thirst, nourishes life, and soothes the skin and muscles. At the same time, it is also powerful, even dangerous, and thus reminds us that we too must die with Christ, die to self and selfishness if we are to be remade and raised up with him.

Lent presents the homilist with a myriad of opportunities to speak about things that really matter, values that really last, life that really is more enduring than suffering and death. Lent depicts the way of the disciple, a way that can be difficult and does demand self-sacrifice, but a way infused with such love that it makes us want to lay aside everything else, every false god or artificial distraction from the reality of God's intense love for us. The heart of the Gospel is here in this season, in a preparatory way that will be fully disclosed in the liturgies of Holy Thursday, Good Friday, and Easter. The preacher's challenge is to lay Lent's invitations before the feet of his hearers in such a way that they will want to respond. At the same time, the preacher must avoid the danger of a Pelagian interpretation—that is to say, any interpretation that smacks of earning God's favor or manipulating the divine will. Our

Lenten asceticism does not earn what God freely gives in this mighty series of narratives. The disciplines we undertake in this season, used properly, help orient the heart, mind, and will toward the divine invitation. When the heart of God opens, who cannot respond but by giving one's heart in return?

The Scrutinies

The Period of Purification and Enlightenment is punctuated by three brief yet poignant rituals celebrated with the elect, normally at the Sunday liturgy. The RCIA describes these rites in this way:

> The scrutinies . . . are rites for self-searching and repentance and have above all a spiritual purpose. The scrutinies are meant to uncover, then heal all that is weak, defective, or sinful in the hearts of the elect; to bring out, then strengthen all that is upright, strong, and good. For the scrutinies are celebrated in order to deliver the elect from the power of sin and Satan, to protect them against temptation, and to give them strength in Christ, who is the way, the truth, and the life. These rites, therefore, should complete the conversion of the elect and deepen their resolve to hold fast to Christ and to carry out their decision to love God above all. (RCIA, 141)

There is, then, a lofty purpose behind these relatively humble rituals, and it has to do with breaking the grip of evil over those proceeding toward full initiation. The RCIA presumes that evil can be a mysteriously stubborn force in our lives and in our world. There is no distinction made here between personal or individual sin and social sin; rather the reality of sin is presumed to have both dimensions. More importantly, though, the Rite presumes that the Christian community can tap into powerful divine medicine for the wounds and disruptions caused by the human capitulation to evil.

The traditional name of these rites, *scrutiny*, is sometimes the occasion of some confusion or discomfort for all concerned. The English word seems to carry a connotation of judgmentalism, or a kind of invasive, microscopic inspection. To avoid these negative implications, it is important to maintain a clear focus on the purpose of the rites. Historically they arose from the community's legitimate need to review the candidates for Baptism, to be assured that their preparation was proceeding in good order, and to confirm that the intentions and dispositions of the candidates were in accord with what the community itself professes through Baptism. This ecclesial need would seem to be behind paragraph 142 of the RCIA:

> Because they are asking for the three sacraments of initiation, the elect must have the intention of achieving an intimate knowledge of Christ and his Church, and they are expected particularly to progress in genuine self-knowledge through serious examination of their lives and true repentance.

These occasions are then marked by the Church's fervent desire to pray for the continued growth and ongoing conversion of the candidates. We would do well to remember also that it is ultimately the Spirit of God who scrutinizes and judges hearts, and this process goes on for a lifetime. As the Gospel's power to search the inner reaches of the human person is brought to bear in a special way upon the elect, it is a reminder to all of us of our common need for protection from evil and an invitation to yield to God's liberating and healing power in our lives. While the Church can and must make a judgment about the readiness of the catechumens, it is a provisional, fiduciary judgment, a judgment made in humility and in dependence upon divine mercy, a judgment that acknowledges that God alone is the ultimate Judge. Even such provisional judgment is, of course, difficult and can be erroneous, in hindsight. Nevertheless, this should not overly trouble us. As Jesus himself noted, the weeds and the wheat grow up together—in the Church and in each of our hearts—and, having done our best, we leave this problem to the divine harvester.

The Church normally celebrates the three scrutinies on the Third, Fourth, and Fifth Sundays of Lent. The Cycle A readings are mandated for these celebrations, regardless of which cycle the current liturgical year belongs to. Structurally and historically, the three scrutinies are linked with three great Johannine Gospel stories: Jesus' interaction with the Samaritan woman at the well (John 4); the healing of the man born blind (John 9); and the raising of Lazarus (John 11). While there are considerable commonalities among these, each of these great texts contributes something unique to the struggle against evil marking this season, as we will discuss below.

The scrutinies then take place after the homily. The structure of all three is similar. The elect are called forward with their godparents. The first movement is to a short but poignant period of silent prayer. The celebrant is to ask the assembly to pray for the elect that they "be given a spirit of repentance, a sense of sin, and the true freedom of the children of God" (RCIA, 152). Likewise, the elect are invited to pray in silence, bowing their heads or kneeling "as a sign of their inner spirit of repentance." A series of intercessions then follows, during which the godparents place their right hands on the shoulders of the elect. Then, a long two-part prayer of exorcism is prayed over the elect. The celebrant prays the first part with hands joined, and the second with hands stretched out over the elect. Given the unhealthy fascinations with "exorcism" in our culture, some explanation of what is happening here will be wise, either in the homily or at another time. This is a "minor" exorcism, not to be confused with the much rarer "major" exorcism performed in the case of demonic possession. Basically, this is a strong prayer for freedom from the influence of the Evil One in the candidates' lives. Finally, the elect are dismissed in the usual way before the Liturgy of the Eucharist begins.

Homiletic Possibilities in the Scrutinies

Even though the scrutiny rites take place after the homily, they offer the preacher a number of special opportunities and challenges. One might say that the scrutinies themselves visibly "preach" not only to the elect but also to the whole community. The preacher's task, then, is to work in tandem with the power of the ritual, helping to unfold the rite's full spiritual power.

Above all, the scrutinies are an opportunity for the preacher to take an extended and probing look at the problem of evil and its antidote in Christ. When done fully and well, the scrutinies have the ability to reach deeply into the interiority of a person, inviting a deep examination of conscience and of the ravages caused by evil and, concomitantly, a deeper opening to the healing and saving power of Christ. The scrutinies' understanding of evil and sin is actually quite penetrating. In accord with Catholic moral tradition, we find in these rites that our attention is directed to both the personal and social dimensions of sin. The personal dimension is obvious and strong as, for example, when one of the possible intercessions for the First Scrutiny prays that the elect "may humbly confess themselves to be sinners," and another prays that "the Holy Spirit, who searches every heart, may help them to overcome their weakness through his power" (RCIA, 153.A). In addition, the rite addresses social sin. For example, in the intercessions for the Second Scrutiny, which pray for release from oppression, "that those families and nations prevented from embracing the faith may be granted freedom to believe the Gospel" and "that those who are faced with the values of the world may remain faithful to the spirit of the Gospel" (RCIA, 167.A). The scrutinies avoid a sharp, explicit distinction between personal and social sin, and it is well that they do. Among other things, this means that no quarter will be found here for using "social sin" as an excuse for personal sin nor for complacency. In other words, all of us have to some extent internalized, and are complicit in, the "isms" of the world that we identify as social sin: racism, sexism, consumerism, militarism, the worship of power, political and economic tyranny, marginalization, and so forth. Rather, the scrutinies demonstrate a sophisticated understanding of the ways we participate in evil and the wide-ranging consequences that participation has for us. A careful examination of the prayers that make up these rites reveals that they evince an assumption that evil deforms the human character, stunts growth, and limits freedom. The homilist may assist both the elect and the assembly in the process of self-reflection by which we make these kinds of practical, personal realizations of our participation in evil.

However, if the scrutinies afford us an incisive and humbling awareness of evil, it is all the more important that the homilist help the assembly see clearly and welcome heartily the power and willingness of Christ to set us free from it. As we saw earlier, the RCIA envisions these as rites of healing (cf. RCIA, 141), and it is essential that the preacher clearly proclaim Christ as the paramount source of liberation from evil. All of the Gospel readings assigned for these days and all of the scrutinies contain prayers that focus the hearer's attention on the unique identity of Christ and Christ's eagerness to overcome the evil that cripples the human condition. For example, the second part of the first form of the exorcism prayer at the Third Scrutiny prays,

Lord Jesus, by raising Lazarus from the dead you showed that you came that we might have life and have it more abundantly. Free from the grasp of death those who await your life-giving sacraments and deliver them from the spirit of corruption. (RCIA, 175A)

The scrutinies are not an invitation to wallow in guilt; they point to a doorway through which we may pass to greater freedom and a more intimate relationship with Jesus Christ. The person of Christ and his power for good must always be central in the preaching that surrounds the scrutinies. The tone is confident, even joyful.

A few comments about the particularities of each of the three scrutinies are in order. In some ways the Gospel text for the First Scrutiny, to take place on the Third Sunday of Lent, is the most complex and offers the greatest number of possible thematic approaches for the homilist. The text initially shocks: Jesus is conversing with a woman who is a Samaritan, thus trespassing two social taboos at once. The very nature of the encounter underlines Jesus' mission to reach beyond boundaries and borders into the typically defined margins of human society. Every person is a child of God and thus worthy of Jesus' interest.

Beyond the fact that the Samaritan woman was a social outcast, as far as Jews were concerned, how are we supposed to see her? The usual interpretation has been to see her multiple marriages and her current living arrangement as evidence of personal sin, an interpretation the text of the rite seems to presume when it offers an intercession "that, like the woman of Samaria, our elect may review their lives before Christ and acknowledge their sins" (RCIA, 153.B). A somewhat more benign and elastic interpretation may be warranted, however. The Gospel reading provides no reason nor explanation for the bare facts of the woman's life situation. The facts presented about the woman's life history may simply be intended to impress upon the reader that her life was a mess, a narrative with many crooked turns, a life story that, for whatever reason, did not conform to standard social expectations regarding marriage and family. An argument can be made that the Samaritan woman represents both personal sinfulness and social victimization, realities that often tangle themselves together in human life stories. The tenor of the woman's remarks in the highly stylized Johannine dialogue with Jesus seems to accent not so much personal guilt as a twisting path of seemingly fruitless search for home, for meaning, and so on. In this interpretation, then, the woman would seem to represent the existential human longing for not only freedom from guilt, but for positive life meaning and freedom from social structures that fell heaviest upon women and social outcasts. This interpretation seems to inform the first form of the prayer of exorcism, which speaks of the elect "who, like the woman of Samaria, thirst for living water." The homilist may thus propose the Samaritan woman to the gathered assembly as an image of a life story gone awry, who nonetheless merits from Jesus not disdain nor condemnation but an invitation to address her deepest yearnings. The homilist will want to take careful note that this fascinating conversation takes place at a well, in the middle of a thirsty day for both Jesus and the woman. There is thus a baptismal foreshadowing here. The life that Jesus offers us is like the slaking of a deep thirst. It is a conversion story; once the woman has put her faith in Jesus, she is remade into a witness to others, a clear implication of discipleship.

The Fourth Sunday of Lent, in conjunction with the Second Scrutiny, gives us the man born blind who is given sight by Jesus. In some ways, this text lends itself to a social interpretation of evil more readily than the other two, in that Jesus firmly rejects the popular understanding that the man's disability is somehow the consequence of his sin or the sin of his parents. The man is without guilt, and once again the Gospel passage provides no explanation for his blindness. Yet he too becomes a symbol for the human condition and an occasion for a crystallizing demonstration of Jesus' identity and mission. In the highly metaphorical world of the Gospel of John, we are to see that blindness afflicts all of us. Some forms of it are circumstantial, as with the man born blind, while other forms are deliberate, as in the case of the Pharisees who are quick to level unwarranted, self-righteous judgments. Thus the antidote, faith in Jesus, is a kind of sight. Those who can see rightly into Jesus' character, intention, purposes, and identity also receive an ability to see into themselves and into the world. The homilist can take this occasion to speak about sin as willful blindness, of course, but doing so exclusively would seem to narrow the text's message and possibly miss its core. The larger message is that Jesus came to address all that constricts our vision or limits our God-intended role as human agents. The healed man is a figure of social courage both before and after his healing. The source of the man's healing, and thus the source of our own healing, is the person of Jesus of Christ, full of compassion and endowed with power to rout the most stubborn impositions of constricted vision.

The most dramatic pre-Passion Johannine text is saved for the Fifth Sunday of Lent and the Third Scrutiny. In the raising of Lazarus from the dead, we have a direct and immediate forecast of the climax of Christ's own story, the Easter story of his resurrection. However, as is typical with John's Gospel, the sign value of what is happening has multiple layers. In Lazarus' death and rising, we see not only the coming Christ event—we also see ourselves. Sin, and the unredeemed human situation generally, is represented as a kind of death before which we human beings are utterly powerless. Standing before this situation, Jesus is moved with deep compassion and love for us, his friends. Where we are powerless and entombed, he brings his unique power for life to bear. If even death wilts in his grasp, then there is no limit to the power he can exercise on our behalf. Even our final physical death—from which Lazarus has received only a temporary reprieve, after all—does not carry with it the finality we had assumed it carried. Lazarus represents death's assumed finality and represents the human condition at its most desperate and apparently hopeless. Jesus, by way of contrast, holds the power of life itself, wielded for our good. As the homilist stands before an assembly, which knows many brushes with death and apparently deathlike experiences, he will join the text in lifting Christ up as the one who can release us from all death-dealing forces and who promises an ultimate victory over death. No evil, not even the ultimate evil of death, is stronger than his power for life.

The Presentations

The RCIA also envisions two ritual presentations to the elect of two texts, the Creed and the Lord's Prayer, calling them "ancient texts that have always been regarded as expressing the heart of the Church's faith and prayer" (RCIA, 147). It continues, "These texts are presented in order to enlighten the elect." This explanation is so terse as to be puzzling. The sense here would seem to be that these texts, in different ways, are so important to the faith of Christians that their ritual "handing over" constitutes another gesture by which the elect are seen to be proceeding along the path toward full membership. Both texts can be prompts for the kind of fruitful spiritual reflection the Period of Purification and Enlightenment invites. Both should be committed to memory.

The RCIA envisions these ritual presentations to occur in a communal celebration, but outside of the Sunday liturgy. The presentation of the Creed is to take place during the week following the First Scrutiny, and the presentation of the Lord's Prayer during the week following the Third Scrutiny, although "for pastoral reasons" these presentations may be done earlier, during the catechumenate (RCIA, 147). While the setting for both rituals is "preferably" within a Mass, they may be done at a special celebration of the Word. Special readings are assigned that take the place of the weekday Lectionary readings.

If the presentations are done at a non-eucharistic celebration, these could be excellent opportunities for well-prepared lay preaching. In any case, in keeping with the purpose of the Period of Purification and Enlightenment, this is not the time for an instructional approach to these two great texts—that should have happened during the Period of the Catechumenate. Rather, the preaching at these presentations should focus on the spiritual enrichment to be gleaned from the Creed and the Our Father, together with the readings assigned for these celebrations. One good homiletic approach, for example, might focus on the "handing over" ritual gesture, following what Paul says to the Corinthians: "For I received from the Lord what I also handed on to you" (1 Corinthians 11:23). The Creed and the Lord's Prayer summarize what we ourselves have been given by those who shared the faith with us, and now we hand it on to you, the elect, who in turn will hand it on to still others. Moreover, in both cases the preacher can emphasize that both the narrative of salvation history summarized by the Creed, and the essence of the address of God as "*Abba* / Father" in the Lord's Prayer, are precisely for our benefit as hearers and invite a deepening of faith in a relationship of trust with God.

Holy Thursday, Good Friday, and Holy Saturday

The elect should certainly be strongly encouraged, if not expected, to attend the Holy Thursday and Good Friday liturgies, since together with the Easter Vigil the three liturgies should be understood as three movements within a single liturgy celebrating the Paschal Mystery. There is, of course, no particular ritual role for the elect on these days, though they should be dismissed before the Eucharist as usual. Likewise, while the homilist on either of these occasions need not speak to, nor about the elect in particular, it would be good to bear in mind that the elect may be experiencing these liturgies for the first time and, in any case, they are experiencing them in anticipation of Easter and their Baptism. Baptismal implications abound in these liturgies since, as St. Paul reminds us, Baptism is always Baptism into the death of Christ. (See Romans 6:3–11, a text proclaimed at the Easter Vigil.) As the intensity of the Three Days builds, the homilies can be a great reminder on these occasions by helping both the elect and the assembly to see the interconnections among the events and ritual elements.

The RCIA text does give special attention to Holy Saturday. It first counsels that the elect "should refrain from their usual activities, spend their time in prayer and reflection, and, as far as they can, observe a fast" (RCIA, 185). In the parish where I served for several years, we actually scheduled a retreat for the elect and their godparents and sponsors, commencing at the conclusion of the Good Friday liturgy and continuing overnight until the afternoon of Holy Saturday. These hours were spent in quiet prayer, simple meals, reflection on the Scripture texts of these days, anticipation of what would happen at the Vigil, and certain preparatory rituals. The holy atmosphere of prayer and anticipation was always palpable and rich during these hours.

The RCIA text encourages that the elect be brought together on Holy Saturday for some optional preparatory rites. Four are listed: the presentation of the Lord's Prayer, which can be deferred from the fifth week of Lent to this day; the recitation of the Creed; the rite of *ephphatha*; and the choosing of a baptismal name. A fifth option exists, too, and that is the rite of anointing with the Oil of Catechumens, a rite offered for any time within the Period of the Catechumenate (see RCIA, 98–103), but which can be celebrated more than once.

Some brief preaching may accompany any of these rites. The homiletic possibilities of the Creed and the Our Father have been discussed above. The rite of *ephphatha*, which is often included in infant

Baptisms as well, echoes Christ's own words in healing the deaf man, "Ephphatha!" that is, "Be opened!" (Mark 7:34). The celebrant touches the ears of each of the elect and says, "Ephphatha: that is, be opened, that you may profess the faith you hear, to the praise and glory of God" (RCIA, 199). This is a beautiful gesture constituting, as it were, a final, climactic intercession for those about to be baptized. The homilist could enlist this gesture and its accompanying words to help explain the process of coming to faith, and the responsibilities entailed by faith. The choice of a baptismal name, if done, can give the preacher yet another opportunity to speak of the way God calls us each by name, and in doing so, calls the whole person into the regenerative life of faith. Finally, the anointing of the elect deploys the rich symbol of oil. The homilist can recall that in the ancient world oil was applied to the skin for at least three reasons:

1. as a sign of being chosen or deputized for a special vocation, as in the anointing of a king;

1. for strengthening, as it was thought to give muscular strength to athletes; and

2. for refreshment, to ease dry skin or other ailments, especially in an arid climate.

Each of these connotations offers symbolic opportunities for the preacher to speak about an aspect of the faith journey of the elect and the promise of Christ's life poured out on us.

Homily 1 ▪ First Scrutiny ▪ Third Sunday of Lent — Year A
Exodus 17:3–7 ▪ Romans 5:1–2, 5 ▪ John 4:5–42
Michael E. Connors, CSC

It's funny how things happen sometimes, isn't it? How seemingly ordinary or casual encounters can peel back our defenses and make us aware of the deeper levels in our souls, the deeper thirsts we carry within us. A thirsty traveler strikes up a conversation at an odd hour of day. It's an hour when normal people are not at the well, suggesting that this woman was rejected by her fellow townsfolk, and so came to the well at a time she expected not to have to meet any of them. As a woman, as a Samaritan, as a social reject, she must have been utterly shocked that this Jewish man speaks to her at all. Jesus willingly and deliberately crosses chasms of gender, ethnicity, and religion. Soon the woman stands laid bare in her isolation and in the twists and turns of her life story. She is known, accepted, embraced in her pain and her deepest thirsts and offered something, a kind of companionship for which we are all made, yet too often do our best to forget or suppress. She leaves the scene transformed, a messenger of good news to others.

Not surprisingly, news like this travels fast. Miserable Samaritans everywhere always seem to be the first to get the memo and understand its importance. Surprisingly, Jesus lingers among this poor lot for two days. I can hear his disciples murmuring, "This was not in the plan. . . ." Even Jesus himself seemed to assume that, when he said in a different context to another woman, "I was sent only to the lost sheep of the house of Israel" (Matthew 15:24). But that house, it seems, is getting bigger. The fellowship of human need, which Jesus has come to address, transcends ethnicity, religion, gender, race, culture, and lifestyle. The rich, the powerful, and the righteous will have to join his company *there*, among the poor, the powerless, and the broken, at the price of rediscovering their own poverty and putting down their jars too.

If there is such hope for a fringe member of an outcast tribe, then where might that hope be reaching out to touch you or me? Do I dare trust it, leave my water jar, and follow it?

What are we thirsty for? A casual observer, I'm afraid, might get the wrong impression of us. He or she might get the impression that our thirsts are for creature comforts, plenty of good parties and good sex, for our sports teams to win the championship, for high grades, which produce good job offers and the finer things in life, for positions of power, and for prestige in eyes of others.

Of course, you and I know that there is more, much more, to our lives than that. We thirst on a daily basis. We thirst daily, if mostly quietly and alone, for families that are whole and at peace. We thirst for real relationships, relationships of trust and depth. We thirst to serve others, in some small way to make a difference in the world. And, if we clear even a few minutes in our frantic schedules, we may even acknowledge a thirst for God, or at least a thirst for some bigger meaning or plan to it all.

Five thirsty travelers will stand before us in a few minutes, our elect, yearning for the water of Baptism. Like all of us, they have at times sought to slake their thirst on the thin promises and cheap goods peddled in the marketplaces of our culture. Now they desire to lay those things aside and drink deeply from the well that Christ offers. We pray for them, and we join with them in their desire for the water that really satisfies.

Lent comes to us each year to arouse our deepest thirsts, to expose what we've settled for, and to offer us the real thing in Jesus. It is a surprising conversation held at a deep well, interrupting our routine and offering us a long, cool drink in the heat of the day. It frees us to say, "Yes, I yearn for something more than a bank account can give me . . . yes, I long for something I cannot even name. . . ."

What is the thirst Jesus names in us this Lent? What is the water he is offering me?

Commentary

The reader will note, in this and the two sample homilies that follow, that the address is to the whole community, not just to the elect. A mistake often made at the scrutinies, and in the other rites of the initiation process, is for the homilist to speak just to the catechumens or to the elect and not to everyone. In the case of the First Scrutiny and the text of the Samaritan woman conversing with Jesus at the well, it is good to remember that the basic metaphors here of thirst and water speak to universal needs in the human condition. The unnamed Samaritan woman represents all of the marginalized, those alienated from God's life by their own sin, as well as those sidelined from society by its norms and expectations. The irregularities of her life story and living situation suggest a restless, perhaps even desperate, search for belonging and meaning. In other words, she embodies a deep kind of spiritual thirst that Jesus recognizes and seeks to address. The homily, then, first explores the narrative of this meeting at the well, seeking to insert all of the hearers, and not just the elect, into the character of the woman. As the woman thirsts for a better life, so do we. As Jesus sees her, recognizes her need, and offers to address it, so he will do for us. As she comes away from the encounter with Jesus changed, and becomes a witness to others, so we too, can be changed and can tell others of the power of meeting Christ at a deep level of our personhood.

The homily also attempts to be frank and probing with regard to our own human thirsts and the often mistaken ways through which we have tried to address, or at least numb, those thirsts. The elect stand before us as exemplars of thirst and sin, but this is not so that we can stand in judgment of them. Rather, like the Samaritan women, they present a mirror into which we are invited to gaze. The goal is to arouse and bring to the surface the longing, the pain, the mistakes, so that the merciful and compassionate knowledge of God can probe us. In a Lenten vein, this homily seeks to bring to conscious recognition our failures and our longings so that we can then present them to Christ. The Good News is that Jesus sees us, knows us, and loves us to a new and better life. From this fairly early moment in Lent, we go deeper into the journey of self-reflection, confident that we will be met by Christ of infinite patience and compassion for our brokenness.

Homily 2 ▪ Second Scrutiny ▪ Fourth Sunday of Lent—Year A
1 Samuel 16:1b, 6–7, 10–13a ▪ Ephesians 5:8–14 ▪ John 9:1–41
Michael E. Connors, CSC

"I've *been* to the mountaintop. . . . I've *seen* the Promised Land!" So said Dr. Martin Luther King Jr., echoing Moses. We all knew what he meant. He opened our eyes too, and our hearts, and our minds. One man's courageous decision to beg for the gift of sight, one community's collective decision to see and name what they saw, peeled back the darkness and made the world, for once, a better place.

Democracy, you know, was supposed to be a structure for better seeing. More pairs of eyes looking at things, more minds in the conversation, more shared responsibility were supposed to produce better decisions, more collective wisdom, and happiness. One might think that we would scour the land for those who can help us see, and beg visionaries to lead us. Yet too often, it seems we continue to elect small-minded people who only confirm our inability or unwillingness to see, who pander to our fears rather than show us how to confront them. "The blind leading the blind," we say. "For lack of vision," the Book of Proverbs says (29:18), "the people perish."

"There are none so blind as those who will not see," says an old English proverb. Jesus encounters a man blind from birth, probably an everyday occurrence in his travels. It is a contrast story—but the contrast is not between the blind and the sighted. The real contrast is between one man's acknowledged incapacity and the willful blindness of nearly everyone else in the story.

The disciples speak for the willful social blindness that is always eager to blame the victim. We make the poor, the unemployed, the sick, and the disabled prove to us that their condition is not somehow their fault.

His neighbors—evidently they haven't really looked him in the face long enough to remember and know who he is. The wretched who beg from us are pushed to the margins of sight, where they all look pretty much the same.

Even his parents are noncommittal, afraid of getting in trouble. A refusal to get involved is a decision not to see.

The Pharisees, as usual, have everything figured out, with no need to consult anybody. Either the guy never was really blind, or he wasn't cured by Jesus, because we all know that only sinners work on the Sabbath. And they certainly are not going to take instruction from an unlettered vagrant.

Ironically, it is the man born blind who already sees more clearly than anyone else, with the eyes of faith.

What was Jesus' answer to all this? Spittle, mud, and water.

He emits a bodily fluid, human flesh to human flesh, as if to say that relationship is his first and best gift. Soon he will pour out his very blood that we might live in eternal intimacy with him.

He gets his hands dirty. He enlists the earth itself—the stuff of which we are made, yet from which we so often recoil—as an instrument of healing. He smears mud as if it were sweet ointment.

Then there is the water. The man is sent to and through water, cleansing, life-giving, thirst-quenching, refreshing, renewing, precious.

Saliva, dirt, and the Pool of Siloam, linked by human touch and word. All elements of what is real, all symbols of the reality God has ordained. "Fidelity to the real"[2] is always our essential challenge.

---

2. Jon Sobrino, *Spirituality of Liberation: Toward Political Holiness* (Maryknoll, NY: Orbis, 1988), 17.

Do we want to see this Lent? Do we want eyes with which to see Easter's glory?

The elect will stand before us in a few moments with a plea for sight. They will say to us, "We have been blinded by sin and selfishness, by peer pressure, greed, and injustice. Lord, we want to see!" And we will respond by praying for them, "Father of mercy, you led the man born blind to the kingdom of light through the gift of faith in your Son. Free these elect from the false values that surround and blind them . . ." (RCIA, 168.A).

Do we want to see? Then we must be faithful to God, faithful to our created humanity, faithful to the humanity of others *all* others. "The glory of God," said St. Irenaeus, "is the living human person."

We must listen to the earth, its rhythms and limitations, its essential goodness and its need for our careful attention. This is to be faithful to our very creatureliness, for we are part of God's creation, not its masters.

We must plunge again into our Baptism, which gives us sight by sending us into Christ's death, and thereby into the darkest, dirtiest corners of earth, to die and rise with him there. We wash again and again, die and rise again and again. Lord, we want to see!

The man born blind receives sight, real sight in becoming a disciple. May our eyes be opened too, in humanity, earth, and Baptism.

Commentary

What does it mean to see with the eyes of faith? Sometimes we praise "blind faith" as the ideal, by which we mean a kind of trust in God, which does not rest upon nor require a clear, full understanding of God, God's ways, God's purposes and actions. The metaphor of "blind faith" certainly speaks to an exigency that is very real and important.

The inverse metaphor also has something to teach us: faith is a kind of seeing, a faculty of insight which we did not have before faith, a faculty we can improve and grow into. The Johannine story of the man born blind, who pleads for sight from Jesus as he passes by, conjures up for us this understanding of faith's power to illuminate not only God, but ourselves and our world. Many things constrain our vision: our own selfishness and obtuseness, as well as social factors that victimize and oppress. Faith in Jesus lights our lives and the path before us.

This homily challenges the willful refusal to see, of which we are all guilty. Its guiding conviction is that our refusal to see constitutes a basic denial of our status as creatures, a negation of our humanity. All sin seems to carry with it an implied insistence on being that which we are not: gods who rule our own realm and determine our own destiny, and who are thus out of touch with the created world of which we are a part. The earthy materiality of the sign Jesus performs in this instance seems designed to restore more than a broken sense of vision — it restores our relationship to the material order of reality. An incarnational perspective on preaching will insist that materiality and rationality are key dimensions of life lived in deep, intimate relationship with God and others. "Fidelity to the real" is the kind of vision we need, and we find it in relationship with Jesus Christ.

Homily 3 ▪ Third Scrutiny ▪ Fifth Sunday of Lent — Year A
Ezekiel 37:12–14 ▪ Romans 8:8–11 ▪ John 11:1–45
Michael E. Connors, CSC

One time several years ago, I was standing at the grave of my paternal grandparents. It was a chilly, windswept hilltop, and night was falling. As I stood there I was unexpectedly overcome with emotion, and I began to weep, almost uncontrollably. It was surprising because both of these grandparents died when I was only six years old, and while I have some misty memories of them, it wasn't like there was a deep and long-lasting bond, nor a recent separation. What I was thinking about that night had as much or more to do with my father. For some reason my mind was telescoping a long span of years that included the difficulties he experienced as a young boy, growing up in poverty in the Great Depression, going off to the Navy, then putting himself through school and starting a career and a family. I wanted to understand my dad, and his parents, and where we all came from. I wanted to understand the dark side of the human condition. I wanted answers to questions. I wanted to share with them. I wanted to hear from them that I had made them proud. I missed them, for reasons I could scarcely name. There is a cold, hard stone rolled over the mouth of the tomb, separating the dead from the living.

I've long gravitated to that one sentence in today's Gospel, the shortest verse in the entire Bible: "Jesus wept." A tearful woman widowed too young once remarked, "Someone should have told me that every marriage ends in either death or divorce." If you have loved, you have almost certainly wept. "See how he loved him." "Jesus wept."

Another time I stood at the grave of my friend John Cross, tragically and oh-so-suddenly killed in a freak accident in his midtwenties, when he and I were both novices. Tears streamed down my face. But even in the depth of my grief I could not resist the power of his memory, his laugh, his human warmth, the things he said to me. John's friendship was a gift, and even death could not take that from me. Could it be that there is a love more powerful than death? At John's funeral the homilist said, "Eventually the question 'How could a good God take John from us so soon?' is transformed into 'How can it be that God could be so good as to give John to us even for a time?'" It took years for the numbness of that moment to melt into gratitude, and while it doesn't entirely take the sting away, something mysterious did change me. John Shea says, "The love that causes our grief is, at root, the love that consoles our grief."[3]

How many times in the midst of some grief, some misfortune, or some personal failure I have railed at God, "Why does it have to be this way?" I still don't have an answer. I don't feel that God minds my ranting, but nor does He seem to need to answer it straight on.

However, here is where I bump up against a curious thing about this Gospel text. Jesus gets word that his dear friend is ill, but instead of rushing to his bedside Jesus tarries two more days where he has been. Then, suddenly, he announces, we're going back to Judea . . . no, not under cover of darkness, secretly, to Bethany, to tend to Lazarus, Martha and Mary, but intentionally, in broad daylight, in full view of the Jerusalem authorities. The disciples' response is predictable: "Are you kidding me? They were just trying to kill you there!" But Jesus is resolute, intent on confronting death, Lazarus' death and his own. It's as if to say, we too must confront death, head on, and not just its symptoms, but real death. Lazarus is dead.

---

3. John Shea, *The Spiritual Wisdom of the Gospels for Christian Preachers and Teachers: On Earth as It Is in Heaven*, Year A (Collegeville, MN: Liturgical Press, 2010), 153.

Jesus didn't need to raise Lazarus from the dead. After all, bringing him back just sentences the poor fellow to a second death. As Martha affirms, Lazarus "will rise again in the resurrection on the last day." This Jesus who weeps before the reality of death — death that spreads grief from Lazarus' stinking, decaying body to his sisters to the townsfolk, down generations and across time and space — the weeping Jesus bears witness that while death is very real, indeed there is a love stronger than death. Lazarus comes stumbling out of the open tomb to add his testimony that Jesus embodies a love that encompasses and surpasses even death.

The elect who come before us today for their third and final scrutiny before Baptism have contended with the forces of death, and they have found in Jesus Christ a love stronger even than death. "Lord, do not let the power of death hold them [or us] back, for, by [our] faith, [we] will share in the triumph of your resurrection . . ." (RCIA, 175.B).

"Lazarus, come out!" The booming voice comes from a face streaked with tears. "The dead man came out, his hands and feet bound with strips of cloth, and his face wrapped in a cloth. . . . 'Unbind him, and let him go.'" There is an echo here of God speaking through Moses to the forces of slavery: "Let my people go."

Friends, as this Lent comes to its climax, let's make a decision to go back to Judea. Yes, to face our difficulties and danger, to face our loss and grief, to face our neuroses and our shadow side, to face our failures and our despair, to face the reality of death, to face the whole sorry, broken human condition of today. We will see who comes stumbling out of the tomb, and we will hear Jesus say, "Unbind them, and let them go."

Commentary

The Third Scrutiny takes place as the excitement and anticipation of Holy Week and Easter are building to a crescendo. The dramatic raising of Jesus' friend Lazarus from the dead makes for a fitting segue from the end of Lent's journey toward the death and resurrection of Christ. In this homily, the invitation is to face death. Death is a multidimensional reality of human life. It is, first of all, the end of physical life, an end which disrupts human relationships and evokes profound grief. We all face this end, and we all face the grief of relatives and friends who are no longer here. Death's very existence is experienced by every generation as a challenge, perhaps even the ultimate challenge, to belief in a good God who authors life. Even before physical death, we also know deathlike experiences, such as relationships that end, projects that fail, disappointments and betrayals, mistakes we make that have far-reaching consequences. In each case, something dies. This homily dares to name these experiences, without dwelling on them. Yet naming these things is one of the more important things we can do as preachers. Our hearers not only find a kind of relief in hearing their own experiences named by clergy from the ambo; they also gain the assurance that in announcing new life and hope, we mean to speak precisely to them, to their real lives, in all their shattered components.

The raising of Lazarus challenges us to follow the example of Jesus and face the reality of death head on. In Jesus' love for his friend, we see a love that both makes death painful and yet makes it also bearable. In Jesus' summoning of Lazarus from the tomb we see both a foreshadowing of the end of Jesus' own story, and a confirmation of his deepest identity as God's own Son endowed with the very power of life and death. Death of whatever kind is not final—resurrection has the last word. Moreover, the promise here is not just a promise for an eternal life in a heaven beyond earth—it is even more. In Jesus' tender humanity, full of love for his friends, we see that even in this life we may witness and begin to partake in a life that surpasses all the deaths we know so well. Not every deathly situation will be "fixed," of course, and the preacher must be clear about what the promise means. Yet the deathly power is broken in the way that God nonetheless provides for us a future. So this homily points to a power flowing uniquely and lavishly from Jesus Christ, but a power that is not simply abstract and otherworldly, but available here and now to release us from what binds us in fear of death. The preacher's challenge on this Sunday is to bring that power to bear on our present lives as well as our future hopes in a believable and tangible way. The preacher need not dwell on the elect, even though ritually the elect do lead us; in their public courage to face death, we too are emboldened. We are not spared grief and pain; we are promised that they mean something and lead some-where, if only we will trust in Christ's power.

The Period of Purification and Enlightenment, the whole community's forty days of Lent, readies the elect and the community for the celebration of the Triduum, the Three Days of the Lord's passion, death, and resurrection. The elect are now ready to approach the font of Baptism.

Chapter 8

The Easter Vigil

"This is the night . . ."

from the Exsultet, *The Roman Missal*, 19

The process of Christian initiation for adults culminates in the celebration of Baptism at the Easter Vigil on Holy Saturday night. This is our longest and most complex liturgy of the year—but also our most important. For the priest, liturgist, or RCIA director concerned with organization, preparation, music, and liturgical "choreography," the Vigil can be a complicated, even overwhelming, challenge. However, for the homilist, and for all of those in attendance, it is a veritable banquet of preaching possibilities. Done well, the liturgy of the Easter Vigil is powerful, moving, and memorable, befitting its rank as "the greatest and most noble of all solemnities" (RM, 2).

The Easter Vigil has six major parts:

1. The solemn beginning of the vigil or Service of Light
2. The Liturgy of the Word
3. The celebration of Baptism
4. The celebration of Confirmation
5. The community's renewal of baptismal promises
6. The Liturgy of the Eucharist

We will examine each segment and its homiletic implications in turn.

The Solemn Beginning of the Vigil or Service of Light

The Vigil normally begins in an unusual place: outside. A "blazing fire" is built outside the church entrance, and those attending are invited to gather there (RM, 8). Fire has multiple layers of meaning in Christian symbolism. It can symbolize faith, burning within, generating both light and warmth for us. It can symbolize the presence of the Holy Spirit, a reminder of the tongues of fire on Pentecost or the pillar of fire that led the Hebrews through the parted waters of the Red Sea. The blessing prayer over the fire specifically refers to it as a "new fire" (RM, 10). We do not borrow flame from an "old" fire but kindle a new one. The idea here would seem to be that something profoundly important is starting over again, beginning anew. The rising of Christ from the dead is the eternally new source of the faith we celebrate every time we gather. Everything in our faith, and the entire liturgical calendar, flows from what we celebrate on this one special night.

Then the Paschal candle is prepared. It is the largest and most visible of the many candles that may mark our worship spaces. The priest traces the Cross, the *Alpha* and *Omega*, and the numerals of the current year, saying, "Christ yesterday and today . . . the Beginning and the End . . . the Alpha . . . and the Omega. . . . All time belongs to him . . . and all the ages. . . . To him be glory and power . . . through every age and for ever. Amen" (RM, 11). Following this, five grains of incense are inserted into the cross on the candle, four at the arms of the cross and one in the middle, with the words, "By his holy . . . and glorious wounds . . . may Christ the Lord . . . guard us . . . and protect us. Amen" (RM, 12). Crucially important Christological claims are being made here, cosmological claims: what Christ has done in triumphing over death exalts him even above time. We look to the wounded and risen Christ for protection.

The Paschal candle is then lit from the fire with the words, "May the light of Christ rising in glory dispel the darkness of our hearts and minds." Now the symbolism of the fire is coming into sharper focus: it is the Easter event, which scatters the darkness. The lighted Paschal candle leads a procession into the church sanctuary, and the candles of all in attendance are lit from it. The deacon, carrying the lighted Paschal candle sings three times, "The Light of Christ," to which all respond, "Thanks be to God" (RM, 15). Once everyone has taken his or her place, and the Paschal candle is put in its place of prominence, the deacon or a lay cantor sings the Easter Proclamation, the *Exsultet*. This is a long and exceedingly joyous prayer of praise, which recounts the sweep of salvation from Adam's sin through the resurrection of the Lord celebrated on this night. The historical sweep of this text goes very well with the sweep of the readings to come in the Liturgy of the Word, offering the preacher a golden opportunity to speak about the consistency, persistence, and magnanimity of God's efforts to overcome sin and death, efforts that reach their culmination in Easter.

The Liturgy of the Word

The nature of the Easter Vigil precisely as a vigil, a night watch, comes more into focus in the Liturgy of the Word. Here we tell the whole story of salvation history, and the pace is meant to be leisurely and reflective. In the historic understanding of the Vigil, the community would gather in the dark hours for a long period of prayer, climaxing with the dawn proclamation of the resurrection. While most of us will probably not try to imitate that original schedule, we would do well to resist the temptations to minimalism or compression of this extended period of reflection that gradually builds in intensity. The story of God's interaction with the human race is long, and on this night above all, we want to grasp the full sweep of God's gracious intentions on our behalf. As many as seven readings from the Old Testament are possible, preceding the Epistle and the Gospel readings, and each has its own psalm response.

Reading 1: Genesis 1:1—2:2

We begin with the creation story. Not only has God been involved with human history; God is the Author of history itself, the Originator of the planet we inhabit and the entire cosmos that surrounds us. Genesis proclaims this truth in an orderly, hierarchical fashion. It is the human being that stands at the apex of creation. Humans are the highest expression of the divine will and the divine likeness. It is only to human beings that God entrusts "dominion" or stewardship of the created order.

As stewards, we are junior partners, even co-creators, although always accountable to the divine intent behind creation. Stewardship does not breed hubris; it requires wisdom, humility, and prayerful communion with the God who still inhabits creation. Moreover, creation is in some sense unfinished, open-ended. God's creative energies continue to flow outward superabundantly, a theme struck more clearly in the response from Psalm 104: "Lord, send out your Spirit, and renew the face of the earth." Baptism is the sacrament of regeneration, the renewal of creation.

Reading 2: Genesis 22:1–18

Abraham's almost-sacrifice of his son Isaac just might be the scariest story in the Bible. The complete Abram/Abraham cycle is above all a story of God's mysterious, unexpected, free, totally gratuitous call and of the complexity and difficulty of human response to that call. God calls the servant to leave behind what is familiar and come to a new land. However one may interpret God's "testing" of Abraham, this story makes clear that the call demands total attention, complete fidelity, to the exclusion of everything else we hold dear. God can ask for everything from us, for everything belongs to God. Faithfulness has its own rewards, rewards we cannot produce for ourselves. Our lives are lived between call and promise. Those elected for Baptism this night now join us in responding to the call and trusting in the promise.

Reading 3: Exodus 14:15—15:1

Of the seven possible readings from the Old Testament, this is the only one that is required. The Exodus narrative is the lynchpin of the entire Hebrew Bible, the foundational story of the Israelite people. This is the story that is retold at every Jewish Passover, and thus the story retold at every Christian Eucharist. The Christ story, the Paschal Mystery of Christ's death and resurrection, is not a different story but rather the same story extended now through history and geography to embrace those who believe. As God once saved a people from slavery in Egypt, through signs and wonders, so through the signs and wonders of the life, death, and resurrection of Christ, God now saves us from every form of slavery. This story reveals God as not only sovereign but as a God of justice whose intent is to go to any lengths to set people free from oppression. The story leaves the hearer full of awe and gratitude, and invites the kind of celebration continued through the responsorial of Exodus 15. Together with us, the elect now seek the freedom only God can give through the waters of Baptism, as the Israelites were freed through the waters of the Red Sea.

Reading 4: Isaiah 54:5–14

The tender intimacy of this reading is not to be missed. The Creator is now "husband" to the people, full of "tenderness," an "enduring love" for them. Amid the shattering experience of the Babylonian Exile, just when it appeared that history had ended, God reaffirms the covenant with the people through the words of Second Isaiah. While the calamity of history is acknowledged, this opens the way to an even more lavish and surprising understanding of the divine mercy and fidelity. This means that even our sin cannot forfeit nor change God's passionate love for us. Some of the elect, like the rest of us, have strayed far from God's ways and known the pain of separation from a life of meaning and belonging. Tonight we celebrate that we have been found, "rescued" as the responsorial from Psalm 30 says, and restored to God's friendship.

Reading 5: Isaiah 55:1–11

Second Isaiah offers us a second comforting text of covenant renewal. The prophet sees that God prepares a sumptuous banquet with which to address our thirst and poverty, two things that the exiles must have known all too well. In response, we are invited to deeper conversion, casting off wicked ways and turning to the Lord's mercy. Perhaps in response to the confusion, complaint, and depression that ran rampant in the Babylonian Exile, the prophet Isaiah reminds the hearer of the mysterious transcendence of God and God's purposes in the world. He exhorts us to trust in the effective, transformative power of God's word to us—this should be of special consolation to preachers too! As with the previous text, the elect and all of us are assured of God's abiding presence with us, God's undying mercy, and God's faithful love for us. In spite of our infidelity, we are promised a life of joy, as the response from Isaiah 12 celebrates.

Reading 6: Baruch 3:9–15, 3:32—4:4

The deuterocanonical prophet Baruch bridges both the prophetic and wisdom literatures. The text is an exhortation to faithfulness to God, who is both the source of all wisdom and the Creator. Wisdom here is personified in feminine form, walking the whole earth but Israel's special companion through the Law. Psalm 19, the responsorial, rounds out the sentiment with its praise of the Law as "the words of everlasting life." On this night, we celebrate that God's wisdom has become specially visible to us through the person of Jesus Christ. The men and women we baptize have sought to join a community that lives by this revealed wisdom of God.

Reading 7: Ezekiel 36:16–17a, 18–28

On the one hand, the later prophet Ezekiel seems sterner than Isaiah, emphasizing the guilt that brought about the tragedy of exile. On the other hand, Ezekiel too is bright with promise of a renewed covenantal relationship, owing to God's generous mercy. Here the prophet conveys a vision of the people's cleansing of their sin in "clean water" God provides. Our tradition has long seen here a foreshadowing of the Baptism we celebrate on this night. However, paired with this external vision of cleansing is a vision of internal renewal provided by a "new spirit" from God, and here the Church sees a foreshadowing of the Pentecost event that is normally associated with Confirmation. In addition, a striking feature of this reading is its universality, conveyed by God's concern for the sanctity of the Divine Name among the nations. The elect, and all of us, have come from the diversity of nations, drawn to this night by the homing desire for cleansing and new life. Here is where the soul's "longing for God," in the responsorial of Psalm 42, finds a home: "Like a deer that longs for running streams, my soul longs for you, my God." Here is where the desire for a "clean heart," voiced in the optional responsorial of Psalm 51, is finally satisfied: "Create a clean heart in me, O God."

Epistle: Romans 6:3–11

This text from St. Paul is perhaps our clearest expression of the connection between Baptism and the Paschal Mystery. This connection is so powerful and important that liturgical planners may even want to consider having this reading, or a part of it, repeated later in the liturgy, in immediate view of the baptismal font as Baptisms are about to take place. So deeply impressed is Paul by our baptismal unity with Christ, he wants the Roman community to grasp that that unity includes Christ's suffering and death, as surely as it does Christ's rising. For Paul, then, there can be no question of relapsing into a life of sin. The net effect here is to give a very serious gravity to what we are about to do at the font. The pattern of the Paschal Mystery—dying many times and in many ways, again and again, each time reborn to some new life—is recognized and consciously adopted as the pattern by which we too live. The font is thus a place of death, a putting to death of an "old self" enslaved to sin, and a place of rebirth to a new and better life. This text should give serious pause to all who approach the font, either for Baptism or for a renewal of what is promised in Baptism. What takes place here is no less than a matter of life and death. The responsorial of Psalm 118 seems to sum up the entire history of salvation we have heard: "Give thanks to the Lord, for he is good, for his mercy endures forever."

Gospel: Matthew 28:1–10 (Cycle A); or Mark 16:1–8 (B); or Luke 24:1–12 (C)

After the reading of the Romans text and the response, the grand "Alleluia" rings out in the church for the first time since Lent began six weeks ago. All of the Gospel texts make clear that the tomb has been evacuated, and the dead man Jesus is now the living Christ. Only in the pericope from Matthew does the Risen Christ himself appear and speak with the women who have come to the tomb. Each of the three Gospel writers brings a particular theological interest to this moment; yet all three agree that the women disciples were the first witnesses and first bearers of this enormous good news. Deep sorrow and disappointment are suddenly, unexpectedly reversed. The shame and guilt of those who abandoned him are broken by the joy that he has triumphed over death. Still, the empty tomb and the various post-resurrection appearances raise as many questions as they answer. There is a mysterious, almost elusive quality to the Gospel accounts. It is really, recognizably him, the same Jesus who came from Galilee to Jerusalem to meet his death; but he is also different, too, somehow transformed or "glorified." What does his resurrection mean for us? He had to die first to get there, and the wounds of his suffering remain, even in resurrection, but glorified. So for us, there is no bypassing the share of suffering that awaits us. Yet he testifies that death will not be the last word, and that he will always accompany us through the deaths we suffer. Calvary neither is erased nor reduced in importance—if anything, the crucifixion is exalted even more as the very means, the passageway to a wholly unexpected new way of living. The accounts are not surprise happy endings; they have, rather, the almost breathless sense of something totally surprising, something incredibly new just begun and still not completely understood—and something utterly essential and foundational to the Christian way of life. The light of Christ's rising illuminates the rest of his story, and ours. The Passover of the Lord has been repeated in a new and universalized way, setting free all who believe.

Baptism

The celebration of the baptismal rite takes place right after the homily. Ideally, the Paschal candle is carried at the head of a procession leading all to the font. The Litany of the Saints is sung. Then the priest sings or says a long prayer of blessing over the water. This prayer again recounts God's saving actions in history, from creation through the parting of the Red Sea down to the flow of blood and water from the side of Christ on the Cross, and implores the presence of the Holy Spirit as the candle is lowered three times into the water. The prayer concludes with a paraphrase of Romans 6: "May all who are buried with Christ in the death of Baptism rise also with him to newness of life" (RCIA, 222.A).

Next come the elect's Renunciation of Sin and Profession of Faith. While the Renunciation is done collectively, the Profession is to be done individually, unless the numbers are too large. Baptism may be by complete immersion of the body, or by pouring of water over the head three times, accompanied by the Trinitarian formula. Immersion is strongly to be preferred, for its totality more clearly suggests the totality of what is being given to God, and the totality of what God promises in return for this solemn commitment. Immediately after Baptism, the candidates are to be clothed in a white baptismal garment and given a lighted baptismal candle. These minor rites help to illuminate the meanings of Baptism: a new life lived in the light afforded by faith in Christ.

Confirmation

Confirmation then follows immediately and is to take place in close proximity to the font, which emphasizes the essential unity between the two sacraments. The prayers of the Confirmation rite focus on the coming of the Holy Spirit, who conforms the human person to the person and pattern of Jesus Christ, assists the person to bear witness to Christ, and strengthens the person for a life of faith and love. The sacrament has two parts: a prayer of invocation of the Spirit prayed by the celebrant with hands outstretched over the heads of the newly baptized, followed by an anointing on the forehead with the Sacred Chrism and the words, "N., be sealed with the Gift of the Holy Spirit," concluded by "Peace be with you" (RCIA, 235).

Renewal of Baptismal Promises and Celebration of the Eucharist

Although Baptism and Confirmation themselves are never repeated, the next step in the Vigil offers the already baptized a Renewal of Baptismal Promises. In a sense, the Lenten preparations of the whole community of the faithful, together with the Triduum celebrations, have been leading up to this moment of recommitment. The presider asks the assembly the same questions as those just baptized, and they reaffirm the centrality of their Baptism as disciples of the Lord. As a reminder of that Baptism, the presider then sprinkles the assembly with holy water. In some locations, this takes the form of a procession to the font, where all touch the baptismal water and bless themselves with it as a gesture of renewed appreciation for the grace of Baptism and purified desire to live it out.

What remains of the Vigil liturgy is the celebration of the Eucharist, according to established patterns but infused by the special joy of this Easter feast. This first reception of the Eucharist by the newly baptized completes their full initiation into the Church. While it would be an appropriate gesture of hospitality for the neophytes to receive Holy

Communion first, after the celebrant, what should strike the observer is that all of us are one at this Table, on an equal footing, all coming to be nourished by the Body and Blood of the Lord so that we can go forth to live this intimate, covenant relationship in our daily lives beyond the church building. The newly baptized are now fully one with us and process in solidarity with us to the Eucharistic Table.

Preaching at the Easter Vigil

The various parts of the Easter Vigil—not only the special rites of the Service of Light, Baptism, and Confirmation, but also the readings, prayers, gestures, together with the elect and the assembled people— all offer the preacher a plethora of preaching opportunities. One of the preacher's special obligations will be to carefully discern, from the ritual and symbolic banquet at hand, the particular focus that this homily to this community at this time will take. This discernment is always incumbent upon the homilist, at every Sunday Mass. It is true that at the Vigil homiletic discernment may seem to be complicated by the wealth of rituals, gestures, and prayers at hand. As a result, many preachers try to do too much, including too many elements in their reflection, stacking too many things into their preaching. As a result, homiletic unity can suffer. It is important to choose a single focus, and make allusions to a limited number of readings, prayers, and ritual gestures, so that the homily holds together coherently. Coherence is vital to effect and memorability.

Perhaps the most important caution to preachers, however, is to remember the reason we gather on this night at all: the resurrection of Christ from the dead. This is the key to this liturgy, indeed, the key to Christian faith and the key to our own life stories. Thus, the Easter Vigil is not a "graduation" ceremony for the catechumens. While the assembly celebrates with and for them in completing their initiation, and while we also recognize their presence as another sign that the Risen Christ indeed walks and ministers among us, it is not their accomplishment we celebrate. Rather, we celebrate the accomplishment of Christ in vanquishing death that makes possible our faith, our faithful living, and our ongoing transformation into the likeness of Christ, under the power of the Holy Spirit. The happy neophytes symbolize for us the power of the resurrection to change lives and call people from death to life. While they have found this power living among us as the Body of Christ on earth, their thanks and joy are really owed to Christ and none other. Our pledge to support them, made in their journey as catechumens, does not lessen now that they take their places among our ranks in the pews.

Thus, Vigil preaching can be enormously diverse. However, it ought to be specially characterized by several things.

First, Easter Vigil preaching must *embrace and proclaim the whole Paschal Mystery*. On this night, we celebrate Christ's resurrection from the dead. It is important to remember that the New Testament references to this event never separate it from Christ's suffering and death. The two events form a unity, shedding light on each other. Easter does not erase the crucifixion; rather, it illuminates the meaning of what took place on Calvary. The resurrection does not stand on its own, for the Risen Christ still bears in his body the wounds in his hands, feet, and side. The new life of the Easter event comes through the passage of pain and death, not around nor in spite of them. The earliest Christians stood in amazement to see Christ among them once again, and this amazement helped them to see the love and faithfulness that impelled Jesus throughout his life and especially through his passion and death. Death's victory is thus hollowed out, made a vessel for a new and glorified kind of life that the Risen Christ now shares with us. Easter preaching must herald this great good news for our lives and help the whole assembly grasp its message and meaning. The Easter *kerygma* makes all the difference in the world for how we see Christ, how we understand our lives, and what we do.

Therefore, second, Easter Vigil preaching should be *characterized by joy*. The "good news" quality of what we celebrate on this night should be unmistakable in the homily. Many homilists seem to find it difficult to convey genuine joy in their preaching. This is not the time to dwell upon our sinfulness, but upon Christ's overwhelming mercy triumphing over the very worst of our sins and reaching far and wide into the human condition. Yet, the Easter message evokes something more than an ephemeral emotion of elation. The homilist must understand the deep and rich character of Christian joy, and be able to distinguish it from counterfeit or superficial notions of joy. It is not "happiness," for example, in the way that word is generally understood and bandied about in our culture. Christian joy, rather, comes from the experience of meeting a living God. It is an overflow of the encounter with the Risen Christ, and once you have tasted its sweetness, nothing else satisfies or substitutes for it. Because it is Christ whom we meet, Christian joy can accept and even embrace the sufferings we endure. On this night, and every time we preach, we want, above all, to point people toward this spiritual encounter. The joy that characterizes the Vigil liturgy, including the preaching, should entice people to open themselves more deeply to meeting this Christ who died and rose for them.

Third, Easter Vigil preaching should be *rooted in a sense of the grandeur of the whole sweep of salvation history*. Although we tell the story of the Paschal Mystery in every Eucharistic Prayer at every Mass, it is only on this night that we retell and savor the full historical sweep of God's action with humanity. Only at this liturgy do we pause to recall God's action in Creation, the Exodus and Sinai Covenant, the Exile and the message of hope of the prophets, all leading up to the Incarnation of God's Son. In other words, we relive the journey of God's People down through the ages as God has progressively revealed his very self to us, climaxing in the life, death, and resurrection of Jesus Christ. The preacher need not—indeed, probably cannot—comment upon every chapter or event of that long history. However, the homily should convey to the listeners some sense that Easter, however unique it may be, did not spring upon us from nowhere, with absolutely no precedent. God has been actively seeking out and forming a redeemed people for ages, a process that culminates in what we celebrate on this holy night. Revelation comes to us historically, and this gives us the assurance that God continues to reveal and redeem, and that each of our personal and collective histories are touched by the divine salvific will. History is neither inconsequential nor vapid; it is the arena of the Divine Presence, always working for our good.

Finally, preaching at the Easter Vigil should be *closely wedded to the meaning of Christian Baptism*. We celebrate Baptism on this night because of Easter. Easter makes possible the new life in Christ that Baptism conveys. Even though Baptism is not the central focus of the Easter Vigil liturgy as a whole—Christ's resurrection holds that place—Baptism is a vivid reflection of Easter's meaning and power. Indeed, Baptism is a sacramental sign of such fundamental importance for our lives that it would be almost unthinkable not to speak of it on this night. Even so, the preacher will take care to highlight Baptism's meaning not just for the elect upon whom the water is poured at this liturgy, but for all of us. The Vigil liturgy invites the entire assembly to approach the baptismal water once again and hand ourselves over to its power, which is the power of Christ himself. Water is among our most fundamental, essential, and multivalent symbols, suggesting cleansing, refreshment, and life itself. The homilist will do well this night to help us again see, feel, experience what an enormous privilege we have been given in our Baptism, and thus invite us to recommit ourselves to discipleship.

Having presided and preached at several Easter Vigils over the years, I can say that doing so is one of the great joys of my priesthood. The symbols, rituals, and meanings are so very rich that I always find this liturgy deeply moving. There is no shortage of things that can be said this night in the homily. Choosing among them, and then finding concrete homiletic strategies by which to help people connect what they are seeing, hearing, and experiencing with their own lives, remain formidable challenges. Trying to meet these challenges, however, never fails to draw me more deeply into the Mystery and leave me changed, thanks be to God.

Homily 1 ▪ The Easter Vigil ▪ Michael E. Connors, CSC

"Why is this night different from all other nights?"

Very simply, tonight is different and special because in it we celebrate nothing less than the turning point of all human history. The faith that the Easter liturgy proclaims for us is that on Easter night, creation began its long journey back, its journey back to the picture of unity and wholeness that we heard in Genesis. Like a comet at the furthest point of its elliptical orbit around the sun, our broken world is beginning to be mended, restored by the triumph of Christ over death.

We are part of that return, as a people, as a community, as individuals. St. Paul says, "Just as Christ was raised from the dead by the glory of the Father, we too might live in newness of life" (Romans 6:4).

However much death is around us, we cannot be killed. However much isolation there is in the world, we cannot be separated. However much sin there still is in us, we can always be forgiven.

Pretty grandiose claims for this night. But are there not multiple, smaller signs in our lives leading us to believe that history hinges on this moment? Why do you believe that Jesus Christ rose from the dead?

I believe that Christ rose from the dead because I know the experience of forgiveness. It is the most humbling grace one can receive. On its strength, I am forced to depend, concretely, not only from God but in relationships with others. It has been shown me, powerfully, concretely within the last ten days.

I believe that Christ rose from the dead because of married couples who beat the odds, who actually give to the other what their vows demand, whose marriages not only survive legally but actually do lead them through the mystery of the other into the mystery of God.

I believe that Christ rose from the dead because of recovering alcoholics and drug addicts, men and women who discover in God and God alone a spiritual power strong enough to call them from the living death of their disease to a new life of sobriety and healthy relationships.

I believe that Christ rose from the dead because of divorced people who begin again, people whose wounds bring healing to another, people whose love for the Church has not always been returned in kind but who love loyally anyway.

I believe that Christ rose from the dead because of a woman I know who once sat, numbed and glassy-eyed in the silence of the crypt, wishing for death, but who today, in spite of the fact that she has many of the same troubles, can say, "I'm so glad to be alive." There is no force on earth, not money enough, no counselor skilled enough, no drugs powerful enough, to overcome the deep darkness of despair and restore life, except the force that rolled back the stone on the empty tomb.

I believe that Christ rose from the dead because of these catechumens who come tonight for Baptism, whose life paths have taken many turns; whose search for meaning has humbled me and their sponsors and catechists; whose goodness and faith are a spontaneous act of generosity toward us as a community, given to us by our God.

I believe that Christ rose from the dead because I have tasted community. In fleeting moments of prayer in the liturgy, in the boisterous camaraderie of the church kitchen, in the sleeves-rolled-up work of a soup kitchen, I have glimpsed a unity among people, which no power on earth can take away from us.

I believe that Christ rose from the dead because of Pat Rybicki. Pat lies in a hospital bed at this very hour, the end of her life approaching. It simply cannot be that the faith, the good humor, and the selfless concern for others, which have already conquered so many deaths, and which sustain her now in her waning hours in the midst of her own Passion — it cannot be that these things will not endure.

I believe that Christ rose from the dead because I have known love. I have heard a friend say to me, "Mike, I love you *here*" — here in my failure, my embarrassing weakness, even my mistrust of the other. The keys rattled, the door swung open, and I met the only jailer I've ever had: myself.

I believe that Christ rose from the dead because in each of my bleakest hours, my bones numbed, and my senses dulled, some senseless flicker of hope reflected off the dark walls of my entombment and led me to a single candle that is the person of Jesus, hands outstretched. No one can take that candle away from me. No one can take that fire away from us.

Commentary

This homily constitutes a kind of personal credo. Speaking to such a great extent from the first person singular is not my usual *modus operandi*, and doing so carries with it certain significant risks. Not only is there a great deal of vulnerability in speaking this way, but there is also the risk of seeming, unintentionally, to call attention to oneself rather than to God and God's action in our lives. Some homileticians advise against personal testimony or personal narrative in preaching altogether. I would counter with two points. First, preaching always involves at least an implied "I." It will be heard by the listener according to what they know about the speaker. It will be probed for personal authenticity and conviction the way any communication is evaluated. So personal testimony is an integral part of preaching, admitted or not. Our God chooses to work incarnationally, through the embodiment of particular speakers in particular circumstances. Second, in this instance I was speaking to a parish community I had served for a few years, a place where I was at home, where I knew many people and they knew me. Many of the people in that community with whom I had grown to have an especially personal relationship were in attendance at the Vigil. This intimacy between the preacher and the community, I hoped, would help to guard against misunderstandings, including the danger of appearing self-centered. In a real sense, I was trusting in my own personal humility, known through long acquaintance, to provide a vehicle for the message that might allow for a different and deeper kind of hearing on this occasion. I could not have given this sort of homily to another congregation in which I was a stranger or with whom I had no ongoing pastoral relationship.

Approaching this homily, I wrestled with the question: What does the Easter story mean to us and why should anyone believe it? Too often, I think, we get to Easter after a long Lent of spiritual exertion, and we treat Easter as a welcome relief with which to put Lent behind us, and put the road to suffering and death behind us. However, this is too facile an approach to Easter. It not only ignores the unity of the Paschal Mystery in our own human experience, it ignores the many questions with which the Easter texts seek to probe us. We can overlook the obvious fact that, on its face, the Easter narrative is a preposterous story. Moreover, those Easter texts often carry within them an implicit message that goes something like this: "This is our testimony, what we witnessed. But don't just take our word for it — experience for yourself that Christ is still alive!" I wanted to pose to myself, and to my hearers, that all-important question: Have we seen him? If so, where? How? Maybe we need to open our eyes wider and recognize him walking our streets today, stalking the corners of our own experience too often unnoticed. Does our faith rest on a fantastic story? on an exercise in wishful thinking? Or does it rest on something more?

The reader will note that this homily deals only tangentially with the Scripture texts proclaimed at this liturgy. That may be a weakness. However, another homiletic conviction I have is that too many preachers do too much dense exegetical work within the homily (it remains important in the preparation of the homily, of course). Hearers then tend to tune out what seems too technical and tedious. What they are really eager to confront is, "What does all of this have to do with me, with my life, with the way I see the world and live?" Faith is a set of lenses by which we see the world, see the "really real," see God's presence and action within and around us. On this occasion I chose to forego a really close analysis of the scriptural texts before us, and concentrate instead on the central question: Why believe this? The catechumens are joining a community that is continually inquiring into the mystery, continually discovering the Risen Lord anew in its life and in the world.

Homily 2 ▪ The Easter Vigil ▪ Michael E. Connors, CSC

There's a little story told about an artist who went to visit a dear friend. When she arrived, her friend was weeping. When asked why, the woman showed the artist a handkerchief, finely woven and very beautiful, and which had great sentimental value. A single drop of indelible ink had ruined the handkerchief. The artist asked for the cloth, which she returned a few days later. When she opened the package, the woman could scarcely believe her eyes. The artist, using the inkblot as a base, had drawn a design of exquisite beauty with Indian ink. Now the piece was more beautiful and more valuable than ever.[1]

We've done our worst, our worst to blot creation with our greed, our violence, and our insatiable lust for more. We've done our worst to forget the baptismal waters that bind us to the thirsty, the outcast, the suffering, to all God's children, friend and foe alike. We've done our worst to ignore goodness, even to silence the voice of God's own anointed servant.

But tonight we celebrate that the Master Artist has not been overcome by our cruelty nor outdone by our carelessness. The Creator has responded with a work whose breathtaking beauty and open-hearted generosity have outdone not only us but even the earlier masterpiece of creation itself. The very inkblot of human treachery has been absorbed into a stunning pattern of still more love from our God, a design for nothing less than the rescue and restoration of the whole of creation. The stain of our faithlessness has been met not with anger nor vengeance, not even with simple forbearance. Rather, it has been embraced and fashioned into an even deeper revelation of who God is and who we are to become. The Cross, our chosen instrument of

---

1. Paul Wharton, *Stories and Parables for Preachers and Teachers* (Abingdon Press, 1986), 60.

violence and hatred, has become God's chosen instrument of grace, reconciliation, and peace.

Tonight we hear the invitation, "Come to the water!" The invitation echoes from the waters of creation, through the Red Sea passage, through the vision of the prophet Isaiah, through St. Paul's reflection on Baptism, through the angel poised atop the empty tomb: "Come and see the place where he lay." Come to the place where life begins anew! Come to the banquet table where your hungers, at last, will be filled! Come to the open arms of the Crucified One who hollowed out death into a passageway to paradise!

And come they do! We welcome Tara, Christopher, and Karen, our candidates for Baptism. Along with their sponsors and catechists, they gave up last Sunday afternoon to gather in final preparation for this night, and I had the privilege of being with them. Their gathering was at once serious, playful, and prayerful. Their thirst for the water was tangible, their hunger for the bread of full communion obvious, and their anticipation of the Easter fire already burned in their eyes. Dozens of others like them stand tonight in nearly all the parishes in this city and beyond.

Why? Why do they come to us? What do they find here? After all, aren't our failures, our hypocrisies, our divisions and pettiness obvious to them? Of course they are. But, remember *Field of Dreams*? "If you build it, they will come." If we invite them to the pool, they will wash and drink. If we seat them at table, they will share the feast. If we welcome them, they will find a home here. If we light the fire, they will warm themselves. If we tell them the stories, they will listen. And if we share with them who we dream of becoming, they will fall in step with us on our journey, and gladly so. Tonight when we smear them with the Sacred Chrism, confirming their intention to be one with Christ and one with us, invoking upon them the strength of the Holy Spirit, may that strong, sweet fragrance remind us all what a precious gift has been entrusted to us in each other.

Tara, Christopher, and Karen will lead the way for us all to come again to slake our parched lips at the clear spring of rebirth. As we approach this font tonight, we will demand of these young people —and of ourselves— answers to questions about what we will resist, what we stand here for, what we will live for, and what we will die for. Then, and only then, as we dared to come forward yesterday to touch the Cross, we may come again to touch the waters that cleanse, heal, and refresh.

St. Paul warned us soberly about this night and its consequences: "Are you unaware that we who were baptized into Christ Jesus were baptized into his death?" (Romans 6:3). Baptized into his death. . . . If we came looking tonight for a happy ending to yesterday's story, this is not it. This is not quick feel-good medicine for our aches and pains. "We have," Paul continues, "*died* with Christ" (Romans 6:8).

Behind me stands our watery grave. Tonight Tara, Christopher, and Karen will lead us to that water, with their profession of faith, with their "yes" to Baptism into his death. The water has been warmed. (I have a stake in this, so I checked.) This water refreshes; it cleanses; it slakes thirst. But, my brothers and sisters make no mistake: this water also floods and drowns. It says to us, there is no resurrection without the Cross, no new life without a willingness to die.

And after Tara, Christopher, and Karen come up out of the water, it will be our turn, if we choose, to renew our baptismal commitment. Will you come to the water? Who should come to this water? Who has the proper credentials to approach this sacred spring?

Come to this water tonight to renew your Baptism if you affirm the goodness of God's creation, and if you wish to re-commit yourself to respect for all human life, to good stewardship of the planet's resources, to preservation of the beauty and wondrous diversity of what God has crafted.

Come to this water tonight if you wish to stand in solidarity with all those everywhere, black and white and brown and yellow, gay and straight, old and young, women and men, who are trapped beneath the dead weight of injustice and who yearn to breathe free.

Come to this water tonight if you are thirsty and hungry and tired from the journey and without shelter, and if you are ready to admit that these things cannot be bought, anywhere, at any price.

Come to this water tonight if you wish to say "yes" to dying with Christ, "yes" to a kind of love which will put you in harm's way and not be understood by others, "yes" to spending your life's blood that some-one else might live.

Come to this water tonight if you can look upon the instrument of capital punishment, and stare into the vacated chamber of death and say, "NO!"

Come to this water tonight if your *Spes Unica*,[2] your one and only hope, is that He lives.

Commentary

This particular homily is rather long when compared with most of my homilies. This may mean that it tries to do too much, compromising unity of focus. The first movement stresses the paschal character of what we celebrate this night, a movement from sin and death to redemption and resurrection. Thereafter the unifying image is the baptismal water and the invitation "Come!" We will explore several aspects of the symbolic, sacramental significance of the water, including one that is often omitted or neglected: the water is a place of death, in union with Christ. This provides the ground for a strong appeal to a sturdy kind of discipleship: we follow Christ not only in what he does and teaches, but right through to his passion and death, trusting that like him we will be raised to new life. The homily then turns our attention to the baptismal candidates who, in a real sense, lead our community procession to the font. There is a tenor of communal humility here as we consider what it means that these people come to join our ranks and say yes to the Baptism we offer and share. The final paragraphs issue a series of invitations to the water and all it means, to commitment or recommitment to what it implies for our living. Here I use a technique that I only rarely use: the grammatical imperative "Come to the water. . . ." The risk of the imperative mood is that it can sound dictatorial, like the words I tell my homiletics student to avoid as much as possible: *should, ought,* and *must.* I relied on warmth of delivery and the radiant goodness of what awaits beyond and through the water to soften the imperative into the inviting, celebratory mood that I wanted here. In retrospect, perhaps the authoritarian ring of the imperative could have also been softened somewhat by the addition of *please,* "Please come to the water. . . ." At the same time, we don't want to overly soften what is

---

2. The motto of my religious family, the Congregation of Holy Cross, is "Ave Crux, *Spes Unica*"—"Hail the Cross, our only hope." This was coined by our founder, Blessed Father Basile Moreau.

being said here, because an active and full-hearted response is being solicited from the hearers.

Homily 3 ▪ The Easter Vigil ▪ Michael E. Connors, CSC

"Why is this night different from all other nights?" "This is the night . . ." we say. This is the night when we gather at an odd hour, for an odd length of time. This is the night when we perform strange rituals done only once a year. This is the night when we initiate new members into our company.

And this is the night when we tell the four great God stories that define our identity, shape who we are as a people, and, most importantly, tell how we look at life and death and the world around us. And we tell all of these stories together, in one fell swoop, in as grand a fashion as we can muster, as four chapters to one book, four movements in one symphony, four legs of the Table at which we sup, four acts of one human drama.

This is the night when we tell the story of creation. God brought something out of nothing. God drew from chaos a magnificent universe of life, wondrous in its complexity and variety. God reflected God's own self in a myriad of life forms, placed there for no other reason than God's sheer playful delight in diversity. What do we know of chaos? Plenty! What do we know of diversity? It sure can be bewildering! But amid that entire dumbfounding menagerie we dare to discern the hand of the Creator, continuing to fashion, shape, mold, and in-spirit us, and continuing to call this creating work "very good."

This is the night when we tell the story of the Exodus. We were victims of oppression, enslaved to the will of others, crying helplessly for justice and relief. And God heard, God noticed, God saw—and God acted. A burning bush, an unseen hand, an angel passing over, a pillar of cloud and fire in our souls led us out of Egypt and delivered us from our enemies. God opened a path for us where there was none, sustained us in the desert, gave us our own place in the world, and sealed our relationship with a solemn covenant making us God's own. God summoned us to freedom and cut the cords that bound our limbs.

This is the night when we tell the story of our Exile and Return. This time the mess was of our own making. Our own indifference, our own willful inattention, our own determination to depend only on ourselves caused us to be estranged from God, estranged from each other. We had left our homeland and awoke to find ourselves in a land we didn't know. Though we deserved no better, and could do nothing to heal our self-inflicted injury, God had other plans for us. We learned that there is a law that is even higher than justice: the law of mercy. We are not permanently shackled to our mistakes. Our sentence has been commuted. A level highway of return is built for us. Not only can we go home again, but we are welcomed there with an embrace, a banquet, and a spotless white garment.

And, most of all, this is the night when we tell the story that encompasses all the others, the story which we tell every single time we gather, but cannot tell often enough nor well enough. Oh, we thought chaos was a sure thing, but found that it was only the messy workbench of creation. We experienced evil as a constant in human affairs, but discovered God's power to rout the foe. We gave up on ourselves after we had made mistake after mistake — only to find our wounds balmed, our drooping backs straightened, our tumbledown house rebuilt.

But surely there was still one thing certain about the life we knew: the journey would end in the cold and dark of the grave. Until, that is, the earth shook this night and the stone was rolled. Is nothing sure any more? No, nothing that we had so darkly assumed. In a world where a carpenter rises to life again, we can assume only possibility, surprise, and life without limits. The instrument of death was not merely swept aside, it was recycled, refashioned into the very source and location of new sort of existence. Death was not simply overcome by God's power — it was hollowed out into a passageway to a better, more abundant life.

Creation. Liberation. Restoration. Resurrection. This is the night! The world as we knew it is no more.

So, brothers and sisters, what are we to do? Here we look longingly into the empty tomb, long enough, wide-eyed enough to let the news sink deeply into us with its full power for amazement and wonder.

We let the joy of this news throttle us, buckle our resistance, confound our minds.

Then, with the women messengers, and with Peter, we must run to tell others. When we go home tonight, having sung our lungs out and smiled ourselves silly and laughed till our sides ache and feasted on rich foods and partied till the cows come home, before we shut our eyes, this is what we must think to ourselves:

We lit the Easter fire and basked in its warmth and light. Yet still the darkness shrouds the world, encircles our camp, crouches in corners of our assembly, drags at the heels of our feet.

We sang the double and triple Alleluias. But the curse of hatred is still shouted across the barricades of Baghdad, Palestine, the racial and ethnic divides of our own society, the gender and sexual orientation divides of our society.

We filled the church with the scent of burning incense and poured out the sweet-smelling Sacred Chrism on the heads of our new members. Yet the deathly stench of oppression still suffocates the nostrils of the marginalized and the poor.

We bathed our catechumens and ourselves in the clear waters of Baptism, slaking our thirst there too. Yet God's creation is still soiled by human carelessness, fouled by human greed, and the specter of thirst for clean water still stalks too many human lives.

We fed at the family Table of the Covenant. Yet still there are throngs of our brothers and sisters who yearn to be included at the Banquet of Life, who suffer the ache of malnourishment for want of love, friendship, or meaning, or even for lack of daily bread.

To them we must go, with the fire, with the song, with the fragrance, with the refreshing waters, with the bread and the wine. We must run to them now—run to them!—for in running to them we run to him, the Risen One. See, he already goes before us to Galilee!

Commentary

This Easter Vigil homily was my most conscientious attempt to grasp and preach from the panorama of salvation history. It sees that history separated into four great chapters or movements: creation, exodus from slavery, restoration beyond exile, and resurrection from death. While distinct, these movements are interlocking, discrete names for four similar initiatives on the part of God. As we gather this night, we gather aware that we stand in a long tradition, a tradition of God's gracious action in the world, and of human cooperation and resistance, reflection and reception of God's action. The resurrection of Christ is the perfect capstone of that history, but it is also what opens us out to the future, giving us hope. Thus, there is in this homily an interplay between rejoicing over what God has done, what God alone could do, and the ways we can participate in, and cooperate with, what God is still doing or wants to do. Notice that there is also a mystagogical quality to this homily; that is, it reviews reflectively the ritual elements experienced by the assembly and extracts meaning from them. There is also a mission thrust to this homily, tying what we do in the liturgy on this night to the needs of the world around us, to the struggles for justice and freedom. The celebration of Easter ought not result in complacency or smugness among us. Rather, it should fan our desire to roll up our sleeves, stand in solidarity with others, and spread the Good News of this night. "Alleluia!" is an expression of joy and a call to action.

If done well, the power of the Easter Vigil can linger for days, weeks, even years, in the minds and hearts of those who participate in it. The season of Mystagogy that follows it, over the weeks of the Easter season, offer us a special opportunity to remember, savor, linger in the glow of the Easter fire.

Chapter 9

Mystagogy

For you were once darkness, but now you are light in the Lord. Live as children of the light. . . .

Ephesians 5:8

The Period of Postbaptismal Catechesis, or Mystagogy, often gets short shrift in parish initiation processes. Easter comes, the goal of full initiation is reached, people get busy with spring projects, and attendance and interest quickly wane, both for the newly initiated and for their sponsors, catechists, and community. As a priest, preacher, and member of the RCIA team, I often felt a letdown myself after the exciting but exhausting days of the Triduum. Often it seemed the neophytes failed to grasp why their continued attendance at special catechetical sessions might be important. All of this is unfortunate because this period can and should be a very rich time of reflection and spiritual deepening for all—the newly baptized and the whole parish community.

The period commences after the celebration of Easter. Although it has no definite termination point, it is envisioned to coincide with the fifty days of the Easter season, which culminates with Pentecost. The *Rite of Christian Initiation for Adults* calls this "a time for the community and the neophytes together to grow in deepening their grasp of the paschal mystery and in making it part of their lives through meditation on the Gospel, sharing in the eucharist, and doing the works of charity" (RCIA, 244). Thus, the matter of this period—the Scriptures, the community Eucharist, and service of others—is basically the matter of the ordinary Christian life, into which the neophytes are now merging. For the newly initiated, this is a season for consolidating the growth that has already taken place and of finding their place among the ranks of the faithful, living out the Paschal Mystery as disciples amid their ordinary daily lives.

The RCIA also expresses a hope that the neophytes will be "introduced into a fuller and more effective understanding of the mysteries through the Gospel message they have learned and above all through their experience of the sacraments they have received" (RCIA, 245). Although the neophytes "have truly been renewed in mind, tasted more deeply the sweetness of God's word, received the fellowship of the Holy Spirit, and grown to know the goodness of the Lord" (RCIA, 245), the assumption behind this period is that further growth is possible as they savor and reflect upon the experience of coming to full initiation. The text continues, "Out of this experience, which belongs to Christians and increases as it is lived, they derive a new perception of the faith, of the Church, and of the world." Mystagogical reflection and preaching, therefore, should assist the newly baptized in developing these "new perceptions" that continue to grow as the faith is lived in practice.

The text also envisions the wider community to be a vital partner in this process. The whole community "should give [the neophytes] thoughtful and friendly help," it says (RCIA, 244). The Rite goes on to note that the neophytes' "new participation in the sacraments . . . increases their contact with the rest of the faithful. . . . The neophytes . . . should experience a full and joyful welcome into the community and enter into closer ties with the other faithful" (RCIA, 246). The process of fully incorporating the newly baptized into the life of the community and into the experience of *koinonia* takes place in this period and must be carefully cultivated. Moreover, this process is reciprocal; that is to say, it has an effect on the community too. The neophytes' full participation "has an impact on the experience of the community. . . . The faithful, in turn, should derive from [this period] a renewal of inspiration and of outlook" (RCIA, 246). The faith and living practice of the whole community is bolstered and deepened by the experience of incorporating new members.

The RCIA envisions the main locus of postbaptismal catechesis to be the Sunday Masses of the Easter season (RCIA, 247). (Indeed, the Rite even allows for the possibility that the Lectionary readings for the Sundays of the Easter season could supplant the regular Lectionary readings, if Baptism has taken place at some time of year other than Easter.) The text stresses the importance of these Masses for the neophytes and their godparents and indeed for the entire community (RCIA, 248).

Mystagogical Preaching

The Period of Mystagogy prolongs the celebration of Easter by savoring what we have celebrated and continuing to reflect on its meaning for our lives. Mystagogical preaching harkens back to the rites already celebrated and seeks to unfold their full meaning. As the newly initiated are merged into full membership and the ongoing life of the community, this season points to the continued presence of the Risen Christ and the work of the Holy Spirit among us. Thus, the key characteristic of mystagogical preaching is its reflective engagement with the community's liturgical experience. However, mystagogy is more than just an explanation of what is happening or has happened in the rituals in which we have we participated. In a sense, the mystagogical preacher seeks to look not so much *at* the rites as *through* them to the world that the rites disclose. By means of a savoring kind of reflection on the rites, the preacher seeks to introduce the hearer more consciously and explicitly into deeper regions of that mystery that invites our faith, indeed our participation. Thus, the mystagogical preacher wants to wring from the experience of the various rites every possible ounce of meaning and motivation for living a life of discipleship. Those various rites, from the Rite of Election through the scrutinies and especially the Easter Vigil, are still fresh in the collective memory, and the preacher will do well to turn to them as he unfolds the singular, unifying homiletic point of any given day's preaching. Those rites are "text" for preaching in the Period of Mystagogy, in a way analogous to the texts assigned by the Lectionary. The spirit of mystagogical preaching is at once joyful yet serious, full of amazement at the mysteries displayed in the rites, yet determined not to let those rites wash over us without changing us, drawing us into the transformation they offer. The sense of celebration that permeates this season arises not so much from the neophytes' arrival at full membership, but rather from a sense of beginning or renewing the life of intimacy with God and service to God that the Risen Christ makes possible for us.

Even a cursory familiarity with the homiletic traditions that marked the first centuries of the church reveals that preaching was very often mystagogical in character. The church fathers were frequently pointing to the rites in which their hearers had participated, expounding the meanings of the gestures, materials, and words. Such preaching was often shot through with a poignant sense of urgency about those meanings, an urgency not only for the catechumens, elect, and neophytes, but also for the entire community. It is as if patristic preachers did not want their churches to miss any particle of the very deliberate messages infused into the rites. While we need not, and perhaps cannot, imitate patristic homiletic method and style in all respects, nonetheless we would do well to convey in our own day and context a similar sense of urgency and opportunity for our hearers.

To take just one example, we can turn to Craig Satterlee's magisterial work, *Ambrose of Milan's Method of Mystagogical Preaching*.[1] We know that it was St. Ambrose's preaching that so profoundly impressed the rhetorician from Hippo in North Africa, Augustine. Satterlee draws ten conclusions from his study of Ambrose's preaching method. Briefly, they are:

1. Ambrose's use of the rites is practically inseparable from his use of Scripture. Satterlee says, "Ambrose intertwines passages from Scripture with the step-by-step flow of sacramental actions in such a way that the two become the expression of a single reality."[2] Since Scripture is the very ground of the sacraments, rigidly separating the two would be artificial indeed.

2. Satterlee also states, "the most striking feature of Ambrose's use of the rites of initiation is that the explanations of the ritual actions are given only after the neophytes have participated in the sacraments."[3] Ambrose apparently had several reasons for this approach, all of which seem to spring from respect for the fact that one does not really understand a sacramental action unless and until one does it, participates in it. We may not wish to follow Ambrose on this point,

---

1. Craig A. Satterlee, *Ambrose of Milan's Method of Mystagogical Preaching* (Collegeville, MN: Liturgical Press, 2002).
2. Satterlee, *Ambrose of Milan's Method of Mystagogical Preaching*, 186.
3. Satterlee, *Ambrose of Milan's Method of Mystagogical Preaching*, 186.

at least not entirely. At the same time, Ambrose's preferred method may stand as a caution against excessively intellectualized or scrupulous forms of advance catechesis and tedious, meticulous "rehearsals" of the rites that can stress choreography and appearance over the substance of what is to take place. Should they be given an understanding of what they are moving toward? Yes, of course. It should be a proleptic or anticipatory understanding that invites, indeed demands, participation in order to complete that very understanding.

3. "Ambrose understands that the rites are God's means of giving faith."[4] This means that we do not expect the neophytes to readily understand cognitively what they are going through. The rites have, rather, a surprising emotional and spiritual appeal that ought not be clouded by too much overlay. In hindsight, with the gift of faith, and with the assistance of mystagogical catechesis and preaching, the candidates will comprehend the meanings much more fully.

4. Ambrose's use of the rites is specific, concrete, and authentic to their actual celebration. He draws upon the liturgical experience of specific people at a particular time in a concrete community. His appeal to their memory is full of distinctive details, including the participants' reactions, which he carefully noted.[5]

5. Satterlee emphasizes that for Ambrose, the rites are means to an end—that end being, in short, a new life—and not ends in themselves. His explanations of the rites were not merely to satisfy the candidates' intellectual curiosity; he aimed his explanations at increasing faith and pointing to moral implications for living the faith in a world where that faith would often be misunderstood and opposed.[6]

6. Ambrose believed that the very drama of salvation revealed in the Scriptures is being continued in and through the dramatic narrative of the initiation process. The struggle between good and evil, the passage from slavery to freedom, the overcoming of death by life — all of these themes continue to be played out in the lives of the

---

4. Satterlee, *Ambrose of Milan's Method of Mystagogical Preaching*, 188.
5. Satterlee, *Ambrose of Milan's Method of Mystagogical Preaching*, 190f.
6. Satterlee, *Ambrose of Milan's Method of Mystagogical Preaching*, 191–195.

candidates, giving to the rites an "awe-inspiring"[7] seriousness
of purpose.[8]

7. Ambrose understood that the rites speak by means of symbolic logic,
   which is not the logic of typical rational discourse. The purpose and
   meaning of the rites is disclosed through image and symbol, and this
   meaning unfolds in a different way and over time.[9]

8. Ambrose saw that the rites remain mysterious. This means that their
   meaning can never be fully exhausted, never fully and finally captured by even the most adequate of words. Among other things, this
   allows Ambrose to "pile up meanings" rather than insist on one
   precise definition. More importantly, Ambrose's sense of mystery in
   the rites respects "their inner dynamic: the invisible action of God."[10]

9. Satterlee stresses, however, that despite Ambrose's complex understanding of the rites, that understanding is "not indiscriminate."
   Rather, Ambrose's understanding is shaped by his knowledge of the
   history of the rites, their structure, and the theology embedded in the
   tradition, especially in the Bible. This gives Ambrose actually a quite
   sophisticated grasp of God's action through the "ordinary elements"
   of bread, wine, water, oil, word, gesture, and so on.[11]

10. Lastly, Ambrose was able to bring to the task of interpreting the rites
    an impressive variety of methods, an arsenal of approaches drawn
    from the interpretation of Scripture. These methods included direct
    and uncritical transfer (approaching the text or rite "as if it had been
    written with this audience in mind"), allegory, typology, and analysis
    of authorial intent, theme, and translation.[12]

    The foregoing points are not prescriptive, but merely to suggest
some of the rich possibilities awaiting rediscovery by preachers in
our own time. The mystagogue of today should not consider explicit
reflection on elements of the sacramental rites a waste of time, nor

7. See Edward Yarnold, sj, *The Awe-Inspiring Rites of Initiation* (Collegeville, MN: Liturgical Press, 1971, 1994).

8. Satterlee, *Ambrose of Milan's Method of Mystagogical Preaching*, 195–197.

9. Satterlee, *Ambrose of Milan's Method of Mystagogical Preaching*, 197.

10. Satterlee, *Ambrose of Milan's Method of Mystagogical Preaching*, 197f.

11. Satterlee, *Ambrose of Milan's Method of Mystagogical Preaching*, 198–199.

12. Satterlee, *Ambrose of Milan's Method of Mystagogical Preaching*, 200–203.

should he necessarily presume that the hearer today has been so well catechized that most of the major meanings are already well enough known. Perhaps the single most important lesson to be drawn from Ambrose and other ancient sources is the visceral sense of immediacy with which they spoke about the rites. That is to say, their preaching was deeply infused with a sense of God's immediate and active presence in and through the rites. They conveyed to their hearers that God is here now, ready and willing to act and act in a way that makes a difference in people's lives. For them, sacramental action was not mere window-dressing, an optional extra. Rather, it was a vital and necessary way of participating in what God is actually about doing in the world. While sacraments do partake in the meaning disclosure of symbols, they are more: they also convey what they point to. Moreover, in any case, rituals are for us never "merely symbolic," an unfortunate phrase common in our culture today. There is nothing "mere" about the rites, as if the real thing lies inaccessibly elsewhere or behind them.

The mystagogical preacher is needed by the whole community to help us see, understand, and enter into relationship with the God who reaches out to us through the rites. That preacher will help us see and understand God, see and understand the relationship we are celebrating, and see and understand how that relationship affects the way we live and what we do. For priests, especially, whose ministry, identity, and spirituality are so closely related to the Church's sacraments on a daily basis, mystagogical reflection should come naturally, especially in their preaching during Mass. Our homiletic tradition stresses that preaching is not an interruption in the liturgy, but part and parcel of liturgical worship. One of the ways this unity can be preserved and reinforced is by frequent resort to preaching in a mystagogical vein.

This mystagogical task never ends, and is permanently valid in all seasons and with every Christian community. Indeed, one might even say that mystagogy *is* the Christian life, a life punctuated by sacred rites that we return to, always seeking to extract and live their meaning again and again. As Pope Benedict XVI said, "The mature fruit of mystagogy is an awareness that one's life is being progressively transformed by the holy mysteries being celebrated."[13]

Homily 1 ▪ Third Sunday of Easter ▪ Year A
Acts 2:14, 22–33 ▪ 1 Peter 1:17–21 ▪ Luke 24:13–35
Michael E. Connors, CSC

Just three weeks ago, I had the privilege of standing before you to preside and preach on Palm/Passion Sunday. You may recall that I tried to speak of the passion and death of Christ as "the cost of being free." It was the price Jesus paid for the freedom he discovered and lived in the Father's love, and it is the price we too must pay if we want to live as freely and as joyfully as Jesus lived in service of others. What you did not hear from me (unless I forgot again to turn my microphone off), were the first words out of my mouth at the exit of the church right afterward: "Boy I'm glad that's over so now I can go back to running away from all that." I was at least half-serious.

Perhaps in your own life you may find, as I find in mine, that there are countless ways to run away from that Cross—to avoid bearing it, to ignore its pain in my life and in the lives of others, to deny its incessant claims on my attention and energies. Yet the inescapable fact remains that, like it or not, all of life is Paschal. The imprint of death and resurrection is that deep, whether we are in the church or outside of it, whether we are thinking about it or oblivious to it, whether we stand trembling with faith in the presence of God, or turn our backs on it all because the dark night has been too dark for too long. The pattern is so woven into the fabric of existence that it goes on and on, and surrender to it, in union with Christ, is the way that lies our freedom and our salvation.

Well, fellow runners, there is good news for us in today's Gospel. Two disciples are leaving town, running away from the disturbing events in Jerusalem surrounding their leader. Even after strange reports begin to surface about an empty tomb, they leave the community behind and hit the road. A pressing errand to run several miles from the capital? Family business to attend to in Emmaus? Perhaps; if so, it

---

13. *Sacramentum Caritatis*, 64.

couldn't have been very important because once they meet the Risen Christ the reason for the trip is forgotten and they rush back to the church in the middle of the night. No, I think they were turning tail out of disappointment that they had staked their lives to this Jesus and been proven wrong. I think they were scared witless, and who can blame them for thinking they might be next on the list to be arrested, tortured, and put to death? And here is where the Risen Christ joins them on the journey, not in certainty or faith, not in a moment of courage or conviction, but in weakness, fear, doubt and flight. They were running away from him, and he chose that moment to reveal himself in a new way.

I wonder if Francis Thompson had this story in mind when he penned his famous poem, "The Hound of Heaven":

> I fled Him, down the nights and down the days;
> I fled Him, down the arches of the years;
> I fled Him, down the labyrinthine ways
> Of my own mind; and in the midst of tears
> I hid from Him, and under running laughter. . . .
> From those strong Feet that followed, followed after.

He pursues those he loves. He catches up with us on the journey, regardless of which direction we're moving, and breaks open for us the meaning of the Scriptures, and the meaning of our lives. He is not allergic to pain, guilt, fear, confusion—he steps into them, takes them on deliberately, fashions from their rough stubbornness smooth and sturdy beams and boards for a new way of life.

If in the end it's all about dying and rising, then it's all about Eucharist too. "They recognized him in the breaking of the bread." So we too are drawn here again and again so that he can reveal himself to us, so that we might recognize him, so that we can be nourished for the journey. If we celebrate well, if we yield to its power here, we might then make all of our meals occasions when we recognize him.

However, friends, the reverse is equally true. His real presence here might elude us if we do not allow our lives to be taken, blessed, broken, and given. In feeding, in being broken open and poured out for others, we will come to recognize him and have cause, here as well as in our homes and daily lives, to celebrate that he lives. The Paschal

Mystery is not complete until it is acknowledged, embraced, and lived consciously in us.

Two disciples are on the road, moving in some other direction. The Risen One joins them. He's doing for them what he always did, and what he still does for us: speaking to them, calming fears, igniting hearts, opening eyes. Here at this Table we learn to see him, recognize him, on all the roads of life. To all the places we go, Christ has already gone before us and waits to meet us on the road.

Commentary

Luke's account of the disciples on the road to Emmaus contains rich opportunities for mystagogical reflection for us. The parallelism of the story with the Eucharist is so obvious, and its lesson so powerfully drawn, that preaching on this text almost demands that the homilist attend to reflection on the ritual that gathers us. In this homily, the mystagogical turn toward the Eucharist is only made in the last few paragraphs. This parallels the story itself, in which the Eucharistic overtones of Luke's narrative only become obvious in the closing scene. Yet that apparently sedentary scene is caught up into dynamism and movement of the whole story, as the disciples admit that their "hearts were burning within them" as the stranger unfolded for them the meanings of the Scriptures in relation to the life, death, and resurrection of Jesus. The disciples' immediate return to Jerusalem resumes the sense of movement, but implicitly now the most important movement is not that of the disciples, whether fleeing the capital or hastily and enthusiastically returning to it. Rather, it is the movement of the Risen Christ—going before all of them, proceeding in ways that utterly shock and overturn expectations—that really has center stage here.

Nonetheless, a close reading suggests that Luke has had the Eucharist in view all along. In a sense, the disciples are coming from the Eucharistic community, going about their business or turning their backs on the Paschal Mystery, as we are all wont to do. They reenter the Eucharistic orbit through their pondering and discussion of the events that have shaken their world, and even more explicitly so through the Risen Lord's assistance in probing the scriptural texts. At the table they are made vividly, sacramentally aware of the presence of the One who has accompanied and guided them throughout. The divine initiative comes first; explicit faith is reaped from the sacramental encounter of reenactment. In other words, the whole scene has a kind of mystagogical dynamic to its structure. It leaves the reader or hearer with a profound invitation to look through the various parts of the Eucharistic celebration to uncover a living Christ with us today, teaching us, feeding us, helping us to see the unfolding of meanings in the events of our lives.

Homily 2 ▪ Fourth Sunday of Easter ▪ Year A
Acts 2:14a, 36–41 ▪ 1 Peter 2:20b–25 ▪ John 10:1–19 ▪ Fr. Joseph Ring

With the canonization of Pope John Paul II, we are reminded of the clear voice of a Good Shepherd, guiding our Church through the last years of the twentieth century and into the first years of the twenty-first century. This saint of our lifetime will continue to impact the Church for some time. He wrote extensively, giving us words of instruction and encouragement to be faithful disciples. He spoke words of mercy and compassion to bring healing to our broken world. He spoke words to correct us in the ways of the Gospel. Many times his were words of truth that challenged us, that cut to the heart of many complex matters at the turn of the third millennium. Some could not bear those words, and so some walked away from the Church. Others were drawn by John Paul's words and example, and became followers of Jesus for the twenty-first century. It was not unlike the first century, those exciting days after Pentecost.

Peter stood up, filled with the Holy Spirit, and spoke some stinging words: "You crucified this Jesus whom God had made both Lord and Christ." These words cut to the heart, for they were true. Some listeners no doubt walked away. However, we hear of others who wanted to know what they can do. They desired Baptism; they wanted to repent and be forgiven. They did just that, and received the gift of the Holy Spirit. Peter was quite persuasive that day, for 3,000 people joined their number of believers.

Today we will add four new Catholics to our parish. Four of the six children in the RCIA, baptized but not Catholic, will make their profession of faith to join the Catholic Church. Then the other two children, already baptized Catholic, will join them to complete their initiation in the sacraments of Confirmation and Eucharist. For them, for all of us,

Baptism is that foundational sacrament. At the Easter Masses, we all renewed our baptismal promises. The union of Christ, the bridegroom, is strengthened with his bride, the Church. The fruit of welcoming these children and the sprinkling rite earlier in Mass is that we recall our own saving Baptism and the coming of the Holy Spirit. Through these sacramental graces, we are members of a community of faith, a community of believers; we have been added to the number of believers.

Through the Sacrament of Baptism, we have entered the sheepfold. The Paschal Mystery, the dying and rising of Christ, is now our experience. We have died with Christ, entering the waters of Baptism, to be raised up to new life in him and in the power of the Holy Spirit. We are given a new name by our Lord and Savior, called a Christian now by Christ. We are his followers now, attentive to his voice, his word of instruction, his word of life.

However, this way of life with the Christ, bridegroom and his bride the Church, is not without difficulty and suffering at times. The early Church knew this. In the Second Reading, Peter is writing to a community undergoing persecution and distress. He, they, and any of us who are suffering servants of the Lord, are to be patient in our suffering, for therein is grace. Now let me be clear. If we are not the sufferers, but rather we witness suffering and injustice, it is our task to bring it to an end through our efforts. Yet there are times when we or others might suffer unjustly, and despite all attempts to bring it to an end, we must endure it. That suffering and perseverance for the sake of the Gospel is a sign of our love and fidelity to our bridegroom, Christ, an example of the sheep heeding the voice and example of the Good Shepherd. Through his innocent suffering, we are healed from all our wounds. Whenever we take up the Cross, doing the hard work of justice: the work of charity to feed the hungry, participating in a prayer vigil on the sidewalk in front of Planned Parenthood, whenever we make peace with those estranged from us, offering a hand of reconciliation to those who have wronged us, forgiving a spouse who has hurt you, then we are striving to be faithful to our Baptism. We are entering again and again into the Paschal Mystery, the dying and rising of Christ. Our own suffering aligns us with those who today are enslaved, held against their will, the physically abused, the bullied, or any who are vulnerable for myriad other reasons. As we ourselves endure suffering and act to bring the suffering of others to an end, it is important to recognize that the goal of the Good Shepherd is not to create suffering, but to end it.

What a graced people we are, sheep of the Good Shepherd! The Eucharist today renews us on our honeymoon with the Lord. Here we encounter him who came that we might have life, and have it abundantly. This week, let us be fervent in our prayer, to hear the voice of the one true shepherd, that we may be faithful disciples of the Lord.

Commentary

This homily by a parish pastor was given on the occasion of an Easter season Sunday at which four children were to be "received" into the Church, then celebrating Confirmation and first Eucharist along with two other already baptized Catholics. One of the great strengths of this homily is that it firmly grounds the special events taking place — reception, Confirmation, and first Eucharist — in Baptism. It beautifully unfolds the meaning of Baptism in a kind of imaginative mystagogical way, harkening back both to the community's reaffirmation of baptismal promises at Easter, and to the sprinkling rite done at the beginning of this liturgy. Anamnesis, or sacred memory, is called up for all present. The homily effectively draws our attention to the baptismal grounding of all we do — which is to say, it draws appropriate attention not to what we do but to what Christ does.

The other great strength of this homily is that it firmly links what is taking place at this liturgy, and links Baptism itself, with a robust and challenging portrayal of Christian discipleship. The opening with Pope John Paul II invites our reflection on a great figure of our times who lived discipleship wholeheartedly through some circumstances that were extraordinarily challenging in his time. Recalling John Paul II's memory helps to fortify the hearer with the courage necessary to live as disciples in the challenges of our own lives and day. The effect is a kind of honesty about the possible suffering that awaits us, while maintaining a fundamentally joyful attitude about the relationship with Christ and the life it brings us, which make bearing the burdens of discipleship possible. The homily effectively links discipleship with standing with others who suffer and working to alleviate suffering to the extent we can do so.

Homily 3 ▪ Pentecost Sunday ▪ Year C
Acts 2:1–11 ▪ 1 Corinthians 12:3b–7, 12–13 ▪ John 20:19–23
Fr. Paul Turner

The month of May is getting busier than the month of December. Making Christmas preparations used to drive everybody crazy. Now in May there are graduations, weddings, anniversaries, Baptisms, Confirmations, First Communions, and receptions in addition to Mother's Day to help us lose our minds. If you have a birthday this month, you'll be lucky if anybody remembers. If you ask people, "How are you," they're likely to answer, "Busy."

In today's Gospel, it's hard to know how to react to the words Jesus says to the disciples: "Peace be with you." He says it twice, in fact, "Peace be with you." If we are anxious about many things this month, these words might bring comfort. But when we're meeting ourselves coming and going, peace seems annoyingly far away.

At the Easter Vigil when we celebrated Baptism, we also celebrated Confirmation. I imposed hands on the newly baptized, prayed for the coming of the Holy Spirit, and anointed them with chrism. Then, I said to each of the newly confirmed the same words that Jesus said to the disciples, "Peace be with you." Doing this ritual sounds easier than it really is. The newly baptized were standing here dripping wet and holding candles. I'm always afraid when I say "Peace be with you" and embrace them, that they will either get me soaked or set me on fire. It's an awkward moment, like many other moments of love.

Confirmation is the first time that the newly baptized share Jesus' gift of peace as Christians. Normally we exchange a sign of peace at Mass just before Communion. It signifies our unity in one way before we signify our unity more deeply in the Eucharist. The newly baptized came to the Eucharist for the first time, but they also shared peace as Christians for the first time. We Christians are supposed to be adept at peace.

Peace is an awkward thing, but many of us can remember that a few years ago, there were some advances. Then-President Barack Obama visited Cuba, a country that had been estranged from us for too long. Or think of the series of agreements in which the United States and Russia agreed to eliminate many nuclear weapons in their stockpiles. It is awkward but important to let go of resentments and remnants of the Cold War.

On Pentecost, we celebrate what Christ gave the disciples, the gift of the Spirit, the gift of peace. With that gift he commands us to forgive and to bring a peaceful presence to the world.

In the busy month of May, and at other times in our busy life-styles, it is hard for us to find peace within. But once we do, once we welcome the Spirit that Christ gives, we can help the world find what Christ wished for his disciples, the gift of peace.

Commentary

This rather brief homily by another experienced parish pastor also looks back mystagogically at the Easter Vigil celebration of Baptism, from the vantage point of the feast of Pentecost, which caps off the fifty days of the Easter season. The preacher skillfully knits together Baptism, Confirmation, the coming of the Spirit at Pentecost and in particular the Spirit's gift of peace to believers. There is an undercurrent of gratitude to God, who alone can give this peace, while at the same time, an inclusion of the truth that peace is also a challenge for us, something that shapes our mission as Christians in the world. Without needing to be very explicit, the homily offers us insight into the foundational nature of the sacraments of Initiation in their relation to the Easter event. The homilist begins by tapping into the busy character of his hearers' lives, as a point of entry into the human need and longing for real peace. The homily's succinctness offers the listener just enough to be suggestive and intriguing, not trying to nail down firmly the nature of the peace offered us, but leaving the listener disciple with work to do — to receive the gift of peace from the Spirit, to seek understanding of it in prayer, and to put it into action in service of others.

Homily 4 ▪ Baptism of the Lord ▪ Year C ▪ Isaiah 40:1–5, 9–11
Titus 2:11–14; 3:4–7 ▪ Luke 3:15–16, 21–22 ▪ Michael E. Connors, CSC

At the doors of most Catholic churches, including this one, stand small bowls of water, blessed water, holy water. As you know, it is our custom to dip our hands into that water and spread it on our bodies (✚) whenever we enter a church, as a prayerful reminder of our Baptism. I have to admit that there was a time in my life when I utterly ignored those bowls of water. I would show up, too often late, breeze through those doors where, heart pounding, not from excitement to be in God's presence but from a life lived at breakneck pace. I'd quickly shuffle myself into a pew. Once in the pew with Mass begun, I could safely continue my thoughts about what I was going to do after Mass or later that day. For years those bowls of water stood mutely but faithfully at the margins of my vision, ignored, dimly understood, a message sent but not received.

Today when I enter church I often take a moment to linger at those fonts, to stick my fingers in beyond the first knuckle, to look at those waters, to look through them to see something more. Sometimes I have to resist the temptation to splash myself with that water rather than just touch my head, shoulders, and chest. Why? The water hasn't changed. The fonts are just as they've always been. No, what's changed is me. And what changed me are the opportunities I've had over the years to walk with people preparing for Baptism, especially adult men and women catechumens who seek to join our Church. Their faith, their eager longing for the waters of Baptism have touched me deeply and refreshed my faith. One of the great thrills of my years in ministry has been the Easter Vigil, when I get to wade into the baptismal pool and look up at those chosen for Baptism and invite them, on behalf of all of us, "Come to the water!"

I don't remember my own Baptism, of course. I was baptized as an infant, as most of you no doubt were too. Our tradition of infant Baptism is a beautiful thing. It is a promise made to us by our parents and by the Church and, more importantly, by Christ himself. But, unfortunately, that tradition can lend itself to under-emphasizing the life-and-death meaning of what we do in that sacrament. We can easily take it for granted or overlook its importance, the way I so long overlooked those fonts wisely placed by the Church at every entrance. To witness an adult being baptized is to witness a miracle, a miracle of God's power to reach beyond human sin and confusion, to change lives, to reorder a person's priorities, relationships, and character, and to pull isolated individuals into a community. When we invite those men and women to the baptismal font, what you see are faces beaming radiantly, ready, eager, happy to have that water poured upon them, relieved to have an old life ended and a new life begun.

Today we celebrate the Baptism of the Lord. We recall that Jesus himself went down into the water of the Jordan River to be baptized by John, not because he had need to be cleansed from sin the way we do, but to give us an example, an example of ownership, if you will: God's possession of him and of all of us. Jesus' baptism reminds us that he and you and I are God's beloved sons and daughters, and God is well pleased with that fact. To these waters we must return again and again and again to quench our thirst, to be washed, and to be reminded of who we are. Here the young and the old, men and women, Americans, Iraqis, Mexicans, Sudanese, are all the same in our need for a life we cannot make for ourselves.

A life we cannot make for ourselves. . . . The baptismal waters still reflect possibilities for us. They still overflow with invitations into the heart of God, into the heart of the world and all its peoples. Let's look into these waters today, recall to whom we belong, and dream of who we could yet become, with God's help.

Commentary

Many opportunities for mystagogical preaching exist outside of the Easter season. The Feast of the Baptism of the Lord is only one of the more obvious of such opportunities. This particular homily attempts to bear witness to the meaning of Baptism as many of the community and I have witnessed it celebrated over the years, especially with adults. In the process, two objections have to be overcome.

The first problem we need to examine arises from infant Baptism, whereby most of us have no memory of one of the most important events in our lives. This tends to result in a kind of routine overlooking of the significance and ongoing meaning of Baptism in the lives of most Catholics. We can address the matter by calling attention to experiences we do, in fact, have—namely, the holy water fonts in our churches and the experience of witnessing adult Baptisms. The extraction of meaning from these ritual moments can help us recover the precious nature of the gift of Baptism in our own lives.

The second objection is the puzzlement often occasioned by the baptism of the Sinless One. The baptismal catechesis that most Catholics have received has strongly emphasized the aspect of the sacrament's power to cleanse from sin. However, if Christ was without sin, as our faith professes, why would he need to undergo baptism? He must have had some reasons in mind for requesting baptism from John the Baptist. This presents an opportunity to pull other dimensions of meaning to the fore-front of reflection. The primary one here resides in the voice of the Father, "This is my beloved Son." Baptism for Jesus and for us represents an inti-mate affiliation with God, and it will serve as a lifelong reminder of to whom we belong. Further, Baptism represents the gratuitous divine ini-tiative of which we will continue to be the beneficiaries, the presence of God that will hover over, around, and within us.

The newly initiated gradually merge their way into the mainstream of parish life. If that parish life is vigorous and robust, the neophytes' transition will be smoother. Their gifts and habits of study, prayer, and reflection, cultivated in the initiation process, will find enthusiastic welcome and ongoing support among other members of the community in the various activities provided by the parish. They will continue to be challenged to growth on the path of discipleship. In the final chapter, we will look at some ways of meeting the challenges of preaching to foster ongoing growth in discipleship.

Chapter 10

Preaching for Discipleship

When the Bible speaks of following Jesus, it is proclaiming a discipleship
which will liberate mankind from all man-made dogmas, from every burden
and oppression, from every anxiety and torture which afflicts the conscience.
If they follow Jesus, men escape from the hard yoke of their own laws, and
submit to the kindly yoke of Jesus Christ.[1]

Dietrich Bonhoeffer

If we are to presume that, like Christ who is God incarnate in space and time,
faith emerges in and is exercised through the ambient of culture, then our
problem of faith and culture leads us to other questions. How can we have a
faith that is truly historical (incarnate), speaking to us in and through cultures,
and yet be a faith that is not reducible to cultural imperatives or cultural
immanence? How can we concretely live a faith that is not domesticated
or intimidated, a faith that is not confined to cultural relativism, a faith that
can challenge cultural ideologies and idolatries, a faith that is not
wholly acculturated?[2]

John F. Kavanaugh, SJ

The Parish and Discipleship

In 2012 Sherry Weddell's book *Forming Intentional Disciples*[3] was
published. It is a good read, and provocative, and seems to have
generated considerable discussion in Catholic circles. Weddell's basic

---

1. Dietrich Bonhoeffer, R.H. Fuller, trans. Revised by Imgard Booth. *The Cost of Discipleship* (New York: Touchstone, 1995), 37.

2. John F. Kavanaugh, SJ, *Following Christ in a Consumer Society*, 2nd ed. (Maryknoll, NY: Orbis Books, 1981, 1991), 73.

3. Sherry Weddell, *Forming Intentional Disciples* (Huntington, IN: Our Sunday Visitor, 2012).

161

thesis is that our parishes are largely failing to pass along the faith and produce committed Catholic Christians. She claims,

> There is a chasm the size of the Grand Canyon between the Church's sophisticated theology of the lay apostolate and the *lived* spiritual experience of the majority of our people. And this chasm has a name: *discipleship*.[4]

In spite of the heritage of the Second Vatican Council, which brought forward again the meaning of Baptism and its universal call to holiness and universal call to apostleship, the author claims that this dynamic theology is not touching the lives of most of the people in our pews—not to mention those who drift away or go elsewhere. She concludes, "The majority of Catholics in the United States are *sacramentalized* but not *evangelized*."[5] Weddell draws upon studies that indicate that the Catholic Church in the United States is hemorrhaging at an alarming rate, especially if one looks at the non-Hispanic segment of the Church. Using both statistics and anecdotal evidence, the author paints a sobering picture of what she calls "our present failure to foster the discipleship of all the baptized."[6] As a result, she continues,

> Many things lie in the balance, but certainly these four:
>
> The eternal happiness in God—the salvation—of every human being.
>
> The complete fruition of the Mass and the sacraments.
>
> The next generation of Catholic leaders, saints, and apostles: priestly, religious, and secular.
>
> The fulfillment of the Church's mission on earth.[7]

At the same time, Weddell does find reason for hope in the example of a small number of Catholic parishes where things seem to be going better. From those select parish communities she draws a series of lessons for other parishes to follow.

I read *Forming Intentional Disciples* with great interest and have found it haunting my thoughts ever since. I have some misgivings about both the methodology and the theological perspective of the book. Weddell's measures of commitment and her understanding of

---

4. Weddell, Forming *Intentional Disciples*, 11.

5. Weddell, Forming *Intentional Disciples*, 46.

6. Weddell, *Forming Intentional Disciples*, 77.

7. Weddell, *Forming Intentional Disciples*, 77.

"discipleship" seem to me somewhat narrow and still encumbered by her evangelical Protestant background. For example, the author seems unaware that even our seemingly "deadest" parishes nonetheless continue to produce a small but steady number of men and women whose lives are marked by a deep piety and true virtue. Anyone who has ministered in a parish knows that every parish has its true saints, and they often reside at the margins of consciousness because of their authentic humility. It is also true that very often Catholics do not use the language of "discipleship," or at least not the way that term may be used in evangelical contexts.

Nevertheless, I do think the author is addressing something that is fundamentally real and troubling. Who of us who have spent time in typical parishes have not wondered why we have so many people who just seem to be "along for the ride," but whose faith doesn't seem to vivify them or inform their behavior beyond that hour on Saturday night or Sunday morning? As beautiful as parish life can be, who of us has not wondered if we could be doing something better to lead people into deep and committed faith and into a life of service and active, explicit effort to spread the faith? Who of us who preaches regularly has not longed to lead our people into a transformative, falling-in-love experience with Jesus Christ, the kind of experience that leads into a deeply committed relationship and issues forth in a discipleship ready to serve and suffer? We occasionally see these things as the fruit of our ministry and our parish communities, but all too often we know the pain of parents whose children stop going to Mass or join an evangelical church. We recognize that the world has changed, and the "glue" which held past generations of Catholics together with their Church is just not there anymore, at least not in modern, urban, individualistic America. We experience cultural forces that are corrosive, even toxic, to the faith we love. Simultaneously, we look around and see a small minority of truly energized lay Catholics, many of them doing wonderful apostolic things both within the parish compound and in the "secular" world. What might we learn from them that could inform our ministry for the better?

Some other advocates of parish renewal seem to share Weddell's diagnosis of our situation—namely, that our parishes are failing to nurture the faith at a significant level of commitment. For example,

Fr. Michael White and Tom Corcoran recount their years of frustration with standard parish ministry in *Rebuilt: Awakening the Faithful, Reaching the Lost, Making Church Matter*.[8] They refocused their ministry around the theme of discipleship. As they say: "The Church has a mission statement. Make disciples. That's it."[9]

Another interesting treatment comes from Canadian Fr. James Mallon in his book, *Divine Renovation*.[10] Mallon describes a long-term effort to move his parish from mere "maintenance" to becoming a community driven by "mission." His sense of mission is derived from Matthew 28:19–20: "Go therefore and make disciples of all nations. . . ."

Mallon says, "To be a disciple of Jesus Christ is to be engaged in a lifelong process of learning from and about Jesus the master, Jesus the teacher."[11] But Mallon believes that at present the term can be applied to only a "small minority" of the people in our churches.[12]

A third recent treatment of the parish takes a more positive approach. William E. Simon Jr.'s *Great Catholic Parishes*[13] reflects on four "essential practices" that lead to vitality in parish life. The second practice Simon examines is: "Great Parishes Foster Spiritual Maturity and Plan for Discipleship."[14] The author says that thriving parishes make the pursuit of members' spiritual development a top priority, reflected in their activities and in their use of resources. "Discipleship," he asserts, "is the central focus of vibrant parishes."[15] Of course, the unspoken assumption here is that most of our parishes are not consciously oriented in that direction.

RCIA: An Engine of Disciple-Making

My own experience in initiation ministry over the years suggested the thesis of this book: done well, the rites and processes of Christian initiation can be one of the most powerful engines of disciple-making in

---

8. Michael White and Tom Corcoran, *Rebuilt: Awakening the Faithful, Reaching the Lost, Making Church Matter* (Notre Dame, IN: Ave Maria Press, 2013).

9. White and Corcoran, *Rebuilt*, 39.

10. James Mallon, *Divine Renovation* (New London, CT: Twenty-Third Publications, 2014).

11. Mallon, *Divine Renovation*, 20.

12. Mallon, *Divine Revelation*, 20.

13. William A. Simon, *Great Catholic Parishes*, (Notre Dame, IN: Ave Maria Press, 2016).

14. Simon, *Great Catholic Parishes*, Part II, 55–95.

15. Simon, *Great Catholic Parishes*, 59.

the parish. I've seen it happen. And I'm not just thinking here of the new Christians who make this journey as catechumens, elect, and neophytes. I am thinking of all who play the active role they should be playing in the process: catechists, sponsors, godparents, ministers of hospitality, the whole parish community—and clergy too. Time and again, I have heard people in these various roles report that their own faith was renewed as they walked with the catechumens. The process makes them ask questions about what all of this means for them personally. It brings to their attention aspects of the faith they may have overlooked, or come into contact with as a child, receiving a catechesis that they have outgrown as an adult. The focus on the Scriptures and the celebrations of the various rituals point to a kind of serious, intentional discipleship that may have been hitherto unknown. Faith presents itself as a journey, or a search for meaning, in a way that it has not appeared previously. Adults have typically done enough sinning, bumped into enough obstacles, felt enough of their own limitations, that they can appreciate the light faith affords in a way that made no sense as a child. This is as true for initiation team members and community as it is for the catechumens themselves. People who enter this process seriously are changed by it.

The key here, of course, lies in the "done well" of my central claim. What it means to actually do the total package of initiation ministries well goes beyond the scope of this book, of course. For the moment, it may be enough to say that, at least for us North Americans, our great temptation when it comes to any sort of sacramental ministry is toward minimalism. The very complexity of the RCIA, as reflected in the text itself, provides many parishes with a motivation to reduce the complexity to more manageable size. So what should be a yearlong process, or more, is compressed into a nine-month academic year. What should be a process of personal growth, aiming at conversion, is reduced to a cognitively dominated school course. What should be an all-consuming process around which a parish community orders all its ministries and resources is reduced to another parish program aimed at a select group. Special rites are omitted or done outside of Sunday liturgy, where only a few participate. Three scrutinies are reduced to one, and so on. Too often the mindset is, what, minimally, do we have to do to have this program in place?

What we should be asking ourselves are more maximal questions. Here are some examples. What sort of parish does the RCIA call us to be? What does it mean to be a disciple of Jesus Christ? How best can we share that with others beyond our church doors? What would it mean to be a truly evangelizing community? What would it look like if foot-washing service in the world was our end game; that is, what we hoped every liturgy, every program would call people to do? How can we engage more people in initiation ministry, and in "full, conscious and active participation"[16] in the Sunday liturgy? How can we do the liturgies of the initiation process so well that their power to call all of us into a deeper walk with Christ is fully unleashed? How can we provide preaching and catechesis that move people to response and commitment?

I suggested above that there are some theological inadequacies in *Forming Intentional Disciples*, but that is really a discussion for another time. My biggest disappointment in Weddell's book, and in the other popular parish renewal books mentioned in the preceding section, is precisely here: the remarkable absence of reporting on the profound experience of disciple-making that many others and I have had with the RCIA. Weddell devotes just a page and a half to the RCIA, in which she pleads for "a truly evangelizing RCIA process."[17] Her point is certainly a valid one, and no doubt it reflects the fact that too often RCIA processes are set up but do not really reflect a priority given to an integrated, holistic evangelization effort. They become just another program, or succumb to a kind of mechanical delivery that does not take seriously enough the dynamics of conversion. However, "truly evangelizing RCIA processes" do actually exist in places, and Weddell's scope is limited by her apparent unfamiliarity with places where the Rite is actually working as it was envisioned to work.

James Mallon devotes about three pages of his book to the RCIA, beginning with the stunning claim that "most parishes also witness a dramatic drop-off of almost 50% of the newly initiated in the first year."[18] Nonetheless, he recognized that something potent was taking place in the process, and "the quality of the formation was of a standard

---

16. *Sacrosanctum Concilium*, 14.

17. Weddell, *Forming Intentional Disciples*, 227–228.

18. Mallon, *Divine Renovation*, 229. The source of this statistic is not given.

generally not offered to the parishioners at large."[19] He then set out to provide that sort of formation for discipleship for the whole parish. In the process, he revised his parish's RCIA model to a process that (a) is open-ended rather than rigidly scheduled on the academic year; (b) is consistently focused on the *kerygma*, or basic proclamation of the Gospel; and (c) connects with support structures of a process similar to the RCIA for the newly initiated to plug into after baptism.[20]

Preaching to Foster Discipleship

If "intentional discipleship" is the goal, how might our preaching ministry contribute to that? How can we preach in a way that stimulates hearers to take the spiritual journey more seriously, fostering committed discipleship?

All of the authors examined above include preaching in their field of concern. Sherry Weddell notes a report from Fr. Mike Fones, OP, as to his own preaching with a renewed emphasis on discipleship:

> My preaching has changed over the last few years. I am surprised by how often the Scriptures give me an opportunity to preach on conversion, on the meaning of the cross, on what it means to be a disciple of Jesus, and even on justification! Someone might say, "Well, that's just because you're looking at the Scriptures with that lens, that bias." I would counter with the possibility that, instead, my previous bias, which did not take life-changing conversion seriously, gave me "eyes that did not see" and "ears that did not hear" what I now see and hear so clearly.[21]

The conclusion here seems to be a renewed emphasis on core dimensions of the Gospel. White and Corcoran devote several pages to the importance of preaching.[22] One of the ten bits of advice they give preachers is "Preach the purpose of the message. Preach life-change."[23] "The purpose of preaching," they continue, "is to change lives." Mallon reports that he preaches for 15 to 20 minutes at every Sunday Mass. "The ministry of preaching is key," he says, "and we should take it seriously. It's the biggest

---

19. Mallon, *Divine Renovation*, 229.
20. Mallon, *Divine Renovation*, 230–231.
21. Weddell, *Forming Intentional Disciples*, 223.
22. White and Corcoran, *Rebuilt*, 141–149.
23. White and Corcoran, *Rebuilt*, 144.

bang for our buck in ministry and we need to do it well."[24] Among other things, he advises that in preaching "we need to be intentional about speaking to the entire person—mind, heart, conscience and will."[25] Conversion has to touch all of these regions of the personality. Mallon also cautions that for long-term change of a parish culture toward focus on mission, we will need to preach about the vision of discipleship over and over again.[26]

The topic at hand, preaching for discipleship, deserves book-length treatment. In the foregoing chapters, we have examined some of the opportunities the initiation process presents us with for focusing on discipleship. But, to conclude here, for now I will content myself to four bits of general advice for preachers in initiating parishes who want their homilies to call all of their people to new or deeper discipleship.

1. Tap into the Power of the Rites

By now, the importance of this point should be clear. The rites themselves "preach" everything that is necessary for a life of following Christ. The preacher merely has to unpack the power, bring it to the hearer's attention, and connect it to the hearer's life experience. Don't think of the rites as mere "illustrations" of a homiletic message that somehow rides above or beyond the rites. The rites themselves convey the most powerful and urgent messages that any of us will ever receive. Remember that our Catholic sense of sacramentality indicates that rituals actually convey, or bring the participant into contact with, what they signify. Thus, we can think of them as "text" for our preaching as surely as are the Lectionary readings. When the rites are ignored, or treated in a condescending or utilitarian way, it sends the message that they are not very important, and that the "real" matter lies elsewhere, probably somewhere in our heads. Liturgy's power, on the other hand, is to catch up all parts of us, not just our intellect, but also our bodies, our imagination, our hearts, our wills. A mystagogical dimension to preaching is practically a necessity if we are aiming at a discipleship that is more than merely notional or abstract. Work with your parish

---

24. Mallon, *Divine Renovation*, 124.
25. Mallon, *Divine Revelation*, 125.
26. Mallon, *Divine Revelation*, 255–257.

community to do the rites fully and well. Then step into the ambo confident that God's power and presence are grasping all of us through these ritual moments.

2. Preach toward Conversion and Transformation

In chapter 5, I discussed Rosemary Haughton's work *The Transformation of Man*.[27] Haughton made a careful and enormously important distinction between *formation* and *transformation*. Formation refers to nearly everything the Church does to inculcate and transmit the faith: liturgy, preaching, religious education, spiritual direction, Bible study groups, catechumenal ministry, and so on. Transformation, on the other hand, is pure gift; it is conversion, *metanoia*, a change in outlook brought about in us—not without our cooperation, of course, but a kind of change that we cannot produce in ourselves by our own efforts. The mature disciple is one who has been touched and changed by God. The process of transformation, to be sure, is long term and knows no point of final arrival in this life. The disciple continues to learn, grow, and go deeper into the life of Christ under the influence of the Holy Spirit. Indeed, it is of the very nature of authentic Christian faith that it yearns to keep growing, to keep going deeper, to yield more and more to the Spirit's work of making us like Christ. Faith is not a package of certainties so much as a confidence in the presence of Christ. As such, it is restless, questioning, and ever growing.

Haughton stressed that formation is valuable and good, and that the Church has accumulated a good deal of wisdom about it over the years, but that it is not an end in itself. Too often in the modern or post-scholastic era we Catholics have approached faith as a matter of mere formation: mastery of the creed and catechism, or right indoctrination, to which we give proper assent. Yet not all formation paths are equal. Some seem to leave no room and no need for conversion or transformation, while other formation strategies help to prepare one for transformation, progressively opening the soul to what God alone can give. Preachers need to remember that their ministry of the Word is always in service of transformation, that it seeks conversion of heart, mind, and will—the whole person. Intellectual substance in preaching is

---

27. Rosemary Haughton, *The Transformation of Man* (Springfield, IL: Templegate, 1967).

necessary and important, but alone it does not go far enough. Affective appeal and stimulation of the will to action are also necessary and important, but neither alone goes far enough. The three dimensions work in tandem.

The preacher must always respect the listeners as free subjects, who can refuse what is on offer, but who just as likely are looking for a reason and a way to say that interior "yes" that only they can give to what God wants to do in them. Respecting the person's freedom, the preacher nonetheless unabashedly appeals to the person's native yearning for relationship with the divine. The power of preaching is not coercive, and it goes beyond the purely rational. Homiletic message, method, and style should seek to serve the conversion needs of the assembly.

3. Preach for Encounter

If we want people to become committed followers of Jesus, they have to first meet him—and not a notion of him, not something about him, but the person himself. As Pope Benedict XVI remarked, "Being Christian is not the result of an ethical choice or a lofty idea, but the encounter with an event, a person, which gives life a new horizon and a decisive direction."[28] Our preaching needs to speak about and point to a living Lord, still walking among us and still teaching, healing, routing evil, suffering with and for us, restoring to life. The experience of meeting that living Lord is incomparably sweet, and once you have tasted it, it changes the fundamental orientation of a person's life and the way you look at just about everything. This personal, spiritual experience is what launches someone on the road of discipleship. We should seek this kind of basic mystical experience for all of our people. Indeed, it is the promise of the Holy Spirit. Every homily should leave the listener with the vivid sense that a living God is near at hand, reaching out in friendship. The listener has but to take that hand, in faith.

For those of us who are priests and deacons, one of the essential dimensions of our ordained ministry is that we are spiritual guides for the communities we serve. We guide others to relationship with Christ in many ways—through the sacraments, of course, but also through personal conversations, catechesis, parish committees, and so

---

28. *Deus Caritas Est*, 7.

forth—but never more so than when we preach. Preaching is an exercise of spiritual leadership addressed to a people who hunger for God, hunger for meaning, hunger to be shown the difference that following Christ can make in the living of life. There is no higher compliment to the homilist than the parishioner who says, "You helped me find God."

There are ways our preaching can hinder this encounter with the divine, and ways that it can make it more likely to occur. This topic, too, deserves extended treatment. But here is some basic advice:

- As you prepare a homily, remember what Jesus said to the fishermen: "What are you looking for?" (John 1:38). Start from the assumption that your hearers are hungry for truth, meaning, love, relationship. Point them to authentic forms of those things.

- Appeal to the imagination. Make liberal use of story, poetry, artistic expression, images. Some aspects of the life of the spirit are enigmatic, mysterious, beyond the purely material or narrowly rational. Get comfortable with paradox and invite your hearers to get comfortable with it too.

- Use the languages of spirituality that have worked down through the ages. Our tradition has a treasury of saints, spiritualities, spiritual mentors. There is considerable diversity here, but some commonalities too. Spiritual language has an immediate and relational quality to it; it is not abstract, but experiential.

- Return to the Paschal Mystery again and again. Christian spirituality is inherently paschal: it takes seriously the Good Friday human experiences of suffering and sin, but presses toward the light of Easter, which promises transformation and holds out hope and joy. We discover the divine in the delights of human relationship, in the beauty of nature, and in music, art, and architecture. But some of our most profound experiences of God come unexpectedly through moments of grief, tragedy, and loss, and we meet the face of Christ in the poor, the marginalized, the suffering. The script of the Paschal Mystery is not external; that is, confined to the death and resurrection of Christ. It is the recurring script of our lives, too, and of the earth itself.

- Convey authenticity and urgency. There is no way to fake this. If you're on the spiritual journey yourself, and still actively seeking, your listeners will pick it up. If in your homily preparation you have discovered something important, your preaching will ring with a sense of urgency. If personal investment is not there, people will tune you out, and quickly.

- Respect the limits of words. Remember that Christian life is both kataphatic (the *via positiva*, or way of words, gestures, and images) and apophatic (the *via negativa*, the way of silence, emptiness, contemplation). Say enough to bring your listeners close to the Mystery, and urge them to leap into it, but trust the presence of God in solitude beyond the liturgy too.

4. Preach a Vision of Personal and Social Transformation

In the Catholic understanding, discipleship is deeply personal, but is never a purely private affair. We are summoned to follow Jesus both individually and as a people, and the two dimensions are intertwined. Our personal relationship with the Savior and decision to follow him is embedded within the Church and flows out into the way we conduct ourselves beyond the church doors. We are part of a historical community, and thus we are social actors and responsible citizens of our society and world. As followers of Jesus, we set our compass as he set his, on the true north of the Reign of God. The Reign or Kingdom of God, or the Kingdom of Heaven, is the master theme of Jesus' ministry and preaching, and he never tired of pointing his followers toward it. Think of it as a totalizing spatial-temporal metaphor for God's universalized covenant *shalom*—in other words, for what life is like when God and humans are in harmony, in right relationship (that is to say, justice). The Reign is God's original and future plan for the created order, and as such, it is both already here, breaking into view, and yet to come—sought and embraced in this life, but with its completion hoped for eschatologically. It is not reducible to "going to heaven," although it does ground hope for life beyond death. Yet it also includes a hope for this earth, a vision of our common future in God.

To be a disciple is to collaborate with Jesus in pointing to, and working toward, this vision of God's Reign. That vision inspires not only our personal acts of charity, but our efforts to reform the institutions and systems of this world to more closely approximate God's life-giving plan of relationships based in a justice that respects human dignity, characterized by mercy, and bearing fruit in peace. God's shalom is an entire social ecology, ordered and balanced among its various parts and infused by God's ongoing creative energy. We humans are privileged to participate in that divine creation. Greed, domination, abuse of power, rape of the earth's resources, the marginalization of some— in these and other ways we human beings fail to be God's partners and upset creation's equilibrium. To be a disciple of Christ is to work toward creation's restoration in a society of justice and peace. Catholic social teaching speaks eloquently to this covenant vision so dear to the Hebrew Scriptures, especially the prophets, a vision for which Jesus himself gave his life. Disciples are anointed with that same prophetic spirit, and it causes us to embrace the world's pain and injustice, spending our lives in generous service of all, but especially of those in need.

As preachers, one of the most important things we can do is help our hearers see the vision of the Kingdom of God and its importance for both this life and the next. Good preaching opens up for people vistas of possibility—both personal and social—that flow from following the Lord. We need to fertilize the imaginations of our people, to help them picture life transformed by the grace of God.

5. Challenge

Some preachers seem to have decided long ago that the risk of offending their hearers is too great, and so they stick to themes and images that console and reassure. However, the Good News of Jesus Christ has a double quality expressed in a banner I saw many years ago: it comforts the afflicted, and afflicts the comfortable. We can see this in the life of Christ himself. He was the very embodiment of compassion to the little ones, but to the self-righteous religious leaders he was infuriating. Our listeners instinctively know that they need both, and I for one really believe that if our words are not regularly challenging, hearers will regard our preaching as superficial. People innately want to grow and stretch, and normally will welcome appropriate challenge if they believe we are authentic, seeking their good, and accepting the same challenge ourselves. We can betray their trust in us by inappropriate challenges, like summary condemnations. But we can also betray their trust by refusing to name the challenges by which we go deeper in our following of Christ. My colleague Karla Bellinger did a study of the ways youth and young adults listen to our preaching. One of her surprising findings was this:

> "Go deeper" was a consistent plea from the young listeners in my doctoral study. "Deeper" does not mean to preach a more strident stance against the moral deficiencies of the world. It means to speak to the joys and pains of everyday life. It means to name the graces of how and where God is present. It means to tell the Good News of Jesus Christ. It means to lift the faithful with the gospel message to be better, to be stronger, to be more loving, to be more forgiving—in short, to grow in their abilities to handle the messiness of life in the strength of the Holy Spirit.[29]

Challenge suggests that growth and change are possible, within reach. And that is good news for all of us.

Some other preachers seem to have long ago decided to be challenging, all right, but their challenge takes on a consistently moralistic tone. Moralism in preaching is moral challenge that springs from judgment, not mercy, from condescension or psychological need rather from a graced encounter that is essentially joyful and free. It often comes in "Don't do this . . ." form, full of *shoulds*, *oughts*, and *musts*. Moralism comes in varieties of both ends of the ideological spectrum: the right (usually concerned with sexual morality) and the left (usually concerned with social justice), and either way, it is toxic. I am not suggesting here that a life of discipleship contains no moral challenges —indeed it does, and of such a degree that none of us will ever fully measure up. But we rise to these moral challenges because we have found a relationship with Christ of such life-giving quality that it gives us the spiritual energy and desire to live differently, in a manner more like the example of Christ himself. And that example teaches us that Christ did not dwell overly long on sins of commission, the moral transgressions that mark our lives. Rather, Christ our model urges us to greater levels of generosity, compassion, and service, levels we could never achieve if left to ourselves, apart from this love relationship with Jesus. Obeying a moral code is relatively easy; spending our life's energy

---

29. Karla Bellinger, *Connecting Pulpit and Pew: Breaking Open the Conversation about Catholic Preaching* (Collegeville, MN: Liturgical Press, 2014), 90.

in self-emptying love of others, as he did, is far more difficult. However, it is a way that points to still more life for us as we progressively become more united with Christ.

The challenge that is more typically appropriate to the homiletic moment is a challenge to respond in faith, make a decision to take that invisible outstretched hand offered in friendship, to commit or recommit ourselves to the One coming near to us, to see ourselves and our world differently, after the pattern of Christ's own consciousness of his own Sonship and God's graciousness. Homiletic challenge is a gift of vision: Christ is here and he will help you live as he did, and as you do, not only will you live differently, you will experience even more blessing and deeper intimacy with him. All of us—catechumens, neophytes, old hands—need to hear this again and again.

Go deeper. "Put out into deep water and lower your nets for a catch" (Luke 5:4).

Homily ▪ Twenty-Third Sunday in Ordinary Time — Year C
Wisdom 9:13–18b ▪ Philemon 9b–10, 12–17 ▪ Luke 14:25–33
Michael E. Connors, CSC

Together with many in this church today, I am old enough to remember *Jesus Christ Superstar*. In fact, somewhere I have the original album tucked away; I think it was the first record I ever bought. To tell the truth, there was a moment in my young life when *Jesus Christ Superstar* played a role in my conversion story. It certainly shook up the categories and smashed the images of Jesus I had learned in Catholic grade school, and that caused me to take another look at him.

In hindsight, what is clear is that whatever else it was, that 1970 rock opera was a poignant bit of social satire — not so much about Jesus or Christianity, but about us. It was about our own age's propensity to manufacture "superstars" and heap upon them our gushing acclaim for what they do for us and how they make us feel; for how beautiful or talented they are; for how well they play the game, or for how much pizzazz and sparkle their media personalities exude. As for its treatment of the Jesus narrative, the story line of *Jesus Christ*

Superstar wobbles between serious encounter and slightly tacky superficiality.

Tim Rice and Andrew Lloyd Weber got at least a couple of things right, though. Their hero tires of his friends' thick-headedness, and grows impatient with the thin, self-interested adulation of the crowds. In Luke's text today, Jesus says some things that are hard to hear. These are set in the context of the growing crowds that were traveling with him. The day came, it seems, when Jesus saw through their demands for more free meals, got fed up with their adrenaline-charged excitement about parts of his message — even while they ignored other parts — saw their fickleness and the disaster to which it was inexorably leading. He wheels about in the crowd of paparazzi, fair-weather friends, groupies and hangers-on and pours cold water on them, as he begins to speak with shocking clarity of the cost of real discipleship. "Building projects and military campaigns have costs," he says, "and so too with what I'm inviting you into. . . . Family, possessions, even life itself — all are worth less than God's own friendship." Jesus is looking for more than "rice Christians" or religious consumers. He is looking for more than flag-waving spectators at his parade, browsers on his website, or fans to fill his stadium. He wants real followers, people who do what he does, live for what he lives for, roll up their sleeves and work with him for the mission he has been given. St. Thomas More is said to have died with these words on his lips: "The King's good servant, but God's first." He did not hate King Henry, but his first love and loyalty were to God. Every age of our history is sprinkled with people who made that choice.

Paul's little letter to Philemon, our Second Reading today, illustrates very practically what this will mean. Paul has befriended and baptized Onesimus, a runaway slave. The slave's master, Philemon, is also the recipient of Paul's ministry. Now master and slave are both baptized, both members of the Church, both disciples of Christ. Paul pleads for Philemon to forgive Onesimus and treat him with dignity, even calls the lowly slave a "brother in the Lord" — clearly the message Jesus himself preached. However, forgiveness will complicate everything for Philemon, socially and legally. Ultimately, it could cost him his very standing in society. We don't know how Philemon finesses the bind he is in. What will it even mean for a Christian to own another human being, much less another Christian? It will be centuries before Christians finally reject the institution of slavery, but without ever calling it into question, Paul has kicked away the very foundations of all forms of tyranny. The dilemma of Philemon is ageless: discipleship can be costly. It complicates things because it doesn't play by the rules human beings ordinarily play by.

Elsewhere in the accounts of the Gospel, Jesus urges us not to count the cost of the love we give away. Is it because there is no cost? God's love, after all, is free, unearned, unconditional, and what we give can be no less so. On the other hand, maybe he recommends not counting the cost because, at the end of the day, it will cost everything. To love even one other human being with the selfless love of only wanting what is best for them, costs every bit of possessiveness lurking in the dark corners of our psyches. Love anyway. To work for real justice for all will unmask our own privileged positions and confront our slightest tendencies to use people for our own ends. Work for justice anyway. In other words, love will cost our illusions, our false values, and our selfishness. All for the priceless, incomparably sweet treasure of belonging to him.

To begin as his friends in the waters of the font, to be fed lavishly at his banquet table, lead us to shoulder the Cross he shouldered along the path he trod. Shoulder it anyway. Walk the path too. It leads back to the banquet table. The last word will be spoken at the table.

Commentary

Some Lectionary readings make it easier to speak directly about discipleship than others, and this text from Luke is one of those. Jesus lays down a series of strong challenges in this text. However, taken out of context, this pericope could give hearers the idea that discipleship is all hardship and pain. The preacher will need to walk a fine line here, to honor the text's challenge while bringing forth the Good News that makes that challenge one that can be met, one that people will want to meet.

Sometimes, too, you have to begin by shaking loose some space in the listener's head, so that the text and its message can win a fresh hearing. In this case, I harkened back to *Jesus Christ Superstar*, which did precisely that for me years ago. Understandably, some found its portrayal of a very human Jesus to be not only unbalanced but also irreverent or even offensive. As a work of popular culture, whose purpose was not so much theological as culture-critical, *Jesus Christ Superstar* can be — and has been — judged in various ways. Nonetheless, it undeniably captured something of the popular imagination and served to give some people a fresh approach to the person of Jesus. The Jesus we find in the accounts of the Gospel clearly becomes irritated with some of the people who followed him, for he saw that they were just looking for entertainment or handouts or what Bonhoeffer called "cheap grace." By way of contrast, the Jesus of the Gospels is inviting people into deep, permanent commitment—a way of seeing life—and a way of living that reflect real, personal change. So in this homily I am trying to steer the hearer through the full shock of Jesus' challenge and into the path that holds for us much more than momentary comfort, flimsy reassurance, or baskets of free food. I attempt to do so in a way that is true to the overall method that characterizes Jesus' ministry, namely, not so much a goad as an exhortation, invitation and vision of a better, richer life. While it is important to be honest about what this path can "cost" a person, I am implicitly wrestling here with the question, "How can giving yourself away actually be a freeing, life-giving thing?" Once again, that question can only be answered affirmatively in the context of a real and experienced spiritual relationship. As a preacher, I am seeking to give my hearers an incentive to love in the unstinting, self-emptying way that Jesus himself loves us.

I labored at length over the conclusion of this homily, as I often do. Good endings are hard to construct. One of my homiletic convictions is that good endings are not too tidy. They don't wrap things up with a pretty bow or a neatly packaged take-away. Rather, effective closings leave something unsaid, something for the hearer to do or to continue pondering, either in the Liturgy of the Eucharist or after Mass on the drive home or during the week that follows or, preferably, all of the above. This conclusion is rather cryptic. My hope is that it leads the hearer to a mystical engagement with the Eucharist asking, "What is that word spoken there?" There is no singular right answer to that query, of course. Yet the lavish generosity of the eucharistic banquet speaks for itself, and it makes it possible for us to bear the cost of discipleship.

Christ calls all to friendship with him, and he calls us to do what he does. Those of us who preach liturgically—and especially through the rites and seasons of Christian initiation—have a unique and precious opportunity to invite them into the life-giving adventure of knowing and following him.

Suggested Resources

Church Documents

Benedict XVI. *Verbum Domini*. Postsynodal Apostolic Exhortation. September 30, 2010. Boston: Pauline Books and Media, 2010.

Congregation for Divine Worship and the Discipline of the Sacraments. *Homiletic Directory*. Washington, DC: United States Conference of Catholic Bishops Publishing, 2015.

Francis. *Evangelii Gaudium (The Joy of the Gospel)*. Apostolic Exhortation. November 24, 2013. Washington, DC: United States Conference of Catholic Bishops Publishing, 2013.

National Conference of Catholic Bishops. *Rite of Christian Initiation of Adults*. Chicago: Liturgy Training Publications, 1988.

———. Committee on Priestly Life and Ministry. *Fulfilled in Your Hearing: The Homily in the Sunday Assembly*. Washington, DC: United States Catholic Conference, 1982.

Paul VI. *Evangelii Nuntiandi (Evangelization in the Modern World)*. Apostolic Exhortation. December 8, 1975. Boston: Pauline Books and Media, 1976.

Second Vatican Council. Ad Gentes. Decree on the Mission Activity of the Church. In *Vatican Council II: The Conciliar and Post Conciliar Documents*, ed. Austin Flannery. Rev. ed. Collegeville, MN: Liturgical Press, 1996.

———. *Dei Verbum*. Dogmatic Constitution on Divine Revelation. In *Vatican Council II: The Conciliar and Post Conciliar Documents*, ed. Austin Flannery. Rev. ed. Collegeville, MN: Liturgical Press, 1996.

———. *Gaudium et Spes*. Constitution on the Church in the Modern World. In *Vatican Council II: The Conciliar and Post Conciliar Documents*, ed. Austin Flannery. Rev. ed. Collegeville, MN: Liturgical Press, 1996.

———. *Lumen Gentium*. Dogmatic Constitution on the Church. In *Vatican Council II: The Conciliar and Post Conciliar Documents*, ed. Austin Flannery. Rev. ed. Collegeville, MN: Liturgical Press, 1996.

———. *Sacrosanctum Concilium*. Constitution on the Sacred Liturgy. In *Vatican Council II: The Conciliar and Post Conciliar Documents*, ed. Austin Flannery. Rev. ed. Collegeville, MN: Liturgical Press, 1996.

United States Conference of Catholic Bishops. "Communities of Salt and Light: Reflections on the Social Mission of the Parish." United States Catholic Conference, 1994.

————. *Preaching the Mystery of Faith: The Sunday Homily*. Washington, DC: United States Conference of Catholic Bishops Conference Publishing, 2012.

Homiletics

Bellinger, Karla J. *Connecting Pulpit and Pew: Breaking Open the Conversation about Catholic Preaching*. Collegeville, MN: Liturgical Press, 2014.

Burghardt, Walter J., SJ. *Preaching: The Art and the Craft*. Mahwah, MJ: Paulist, 1987.

Cameron, Peter John, OP. *Why Preach: Encountering Christ in God's Word*. San Francisco: Ignatius Press, 2009.

Connors, Michael, E., ed. *We Preach Christ Crucified*. Collegeville, MN: Liturgical Press, 2014.

————, ed. *To All the World: Preaching and the New Evangelization*. Collegeville, MN: Liturgical Press, 2016.

Connors, Michael E. and Ann M. Garrido. "Doctrinal and Catechetical Preaching," in Edward Foley, ed., *A Handbook for Catholic Preaching*. Collegeville, MN: Liturgical Press. 2016, 124–133.

DeBona, Guerric, OSB. *Fulfilled in Our Hearing: History and Method of Christian Preaching*. Mahwah, NJ: Paulist, 2005.

————. *Preaching Effectively, Revitalizing Your Church: The Seven-Step Ladder toward Successful Homilies*. Mahwah, NJ: Paulist, 2009.

DeLeers, Stephen Vincent. *Written Text Becomes Living Word: The Vision and Practice of Sunday Preaching*. Collegeville, MN: Liturgical Press, 2004.

Foley, Edward, ed. *A Handbook for Catholic Preaching*. Collegeville, MN: Liturgical Press, 2016.

Harris, Daniel E., CM. *We Speak the Word of the Lord: A Practical Plan for More Effective Preaching*. Skokie, IL: ACTA Publications, 2001.

Hilkert, Mary Catherine, OP. *Naming Grace: Preaching and the Sacramental Imagination*. New York: Continuum, 1998.

Janowiak, Paul A., SJ. *The Holy Preaching: The Sacramentality of the Word in the Liturgical Assembly*. Collegeville, MN: Liturgical Press, 2000.

————. *Standing Together in the Community of God: Liturgical Spirituality and the Presence of Christ*. Collegeville, MN: Liturgical Press, 2011.

Joncas, Jan Michael. *Preaching the Rites of Christian Initiation*. Forum Essays 4. Chicago: Liturgy Training Publications, 1994.

Scirghi, Thomas J., SJ. *Longing to See Your Face: Preaching in a Secular Age*. Collegeville, MN: Liturgical Press, 2017.

Shea, John. *The Spiritual Wisdom of the Gospels for Christian Preachers and Teachers: On Earth as It Is in Heaven, Year A.* Collegeville, MN: Liturgical Press, 2004.

———. *The Spiritual Wisdom of the Gospels for Christian Preachers and Teachers: Eating with the Bridegroom, Year B.* Collegeville, MN: Liturgical Press, 2005.

———. *The Spiritual Wisdom of the Gospels for Christian Preachers and Teachers: The Relentless Widow, Year C.* Collegeville, MN: Liturgical Press, 2006.

Tufano, Victoria M., ed. *Scripture Backgrounds for the Sunday Lectionary, Year A: A Resource for Homilists.* Chicago: Liturgy Training Publications, 2016.

———, ed. *Scripture Backgrounds for the Sunday Lectionary, Year B: A Resource for Homilists.* Chicago: Liturgy Training Publications, 2017.

Untener, Ken. *Preaching Better: Practical Suggestions for Homilists.* Mahwah, NJ: Paulist, 1999.

Waznak, Robert P., sss. *An Introduction to the Homily.* Collegeville, MN: Liturgical Press, 1998.

Wharton, Paul J. *Stories and Parables for Preachers and Teachers.* Abingdon Press, 1986.

Christian Initiation

Duggan, Robert and Kelly, Maureen. *The Christian Initiation of Children: Hope for the Future.* Mahwah, NJ: Paulist Press, 1991.

Dunning, James. *Echoing God's Word: Formation for Catechists and Homilists in a Catechumenal Church.* Chicago: Liturgy Training Publications, 1993.

Harmless, William. *Augustine and the Catechumenate.* Rev. ed. Collegeville, MN: Liturgical Press, 2014.

Jackson, Pamela E. J. *Journeybread for the Shadowlands: The Readings for the Rites of the Catechumenate, RCIA.* Collegeville, MN: Liturgical Press, 1993.

Johnson, Maxwell E. *The Rites of Christian Initiation: Their Evolution and Interpretation.* Rev. ed. Collegeville, MN: Pueblo/Liturgical Press, 2007.

Kavanagh, Aidan. *The Shape of Baptism: The Rite of Christian Initiation.* Studies in the Reformed Rites of the Catholic Church, vol. 1. Collegeville, MN: Pueblo/Liturgical Press, 1991.

Lewinski, Ronald J. *An Introduction to the RCIA: The Vision of Christian Initiation.* Chicago: Liturgy Training Publications, 2017.

Morris, Thomas H. *The RCIA: Transforming the Church: A Resource for Pastoral Implementation.* Rev. ed. Mahwah, NJ: Paulist Press, 1997.

Osborne, Kenan B., ofm. *The Christian Sacraments of Initiation: Baptism, Confirmation, Eucharist.* Paulist Press, 1987.

Satterlee, Craig Alan. *Ambrose of Milan's Method of Mystagogical Preaching.* Collegeville, MN: Liturgical Press, 2002.

Satterlee, Craig Alan and Lester Ruth. *Creative Preaching on the Sacraments.* Nashville, TN: Discipleship Resources, 2001.

Searle, Mark. *Christening: The Making of Christians.* Collegeville, MN: Liturgical Press, 1980.

———. *Alternative Futures for Worship: Baptism and Confirmation.* Collegeville, MN: Liturgical Press, 1987.

Stice, Randy. *Understanding the Sacraments of Initiation: A Rite-Based Approach.* Chicago: Liturgy Training Publications, 2017.

Turner, Paul. *Hallelujah Highway: A History of the Catechumenate.* Chicago: Liturgy Training Publications, 2000.

———. *Ages of Initiation: The First Two Christian Millennia.* Collegeville, MN: Liturgical Press, 2001.

———. *Celebrating Initiation: A Guide for Priests.* Schiller Park, IL: World Library Publications. 2007.

Walsh, Liam, OP. *Sacraments of Initiation. A Theology of Life, Word and Rite.* Second edition. Chicago: Hillenbrand Books, 2011.

Wilbricht, Stephen S., CSC. *The Role of the Priest in Christian Initiation.* Chicago: Liturgy Training Publications, 2017.

Yarnold, Edward, SJ. *The Awe-Inspiring Rites of Initiation.* Collegeville, MN: Liturgical Press. 1971, 1994.

Discipleship / The Evangelizing Parish

Gallagher, Timothy M., OMV. *The Discernment of Spirits: An Ignatian Guide for Everyday Living.* New York: Crossroad, 2005.

Greenleaf, Robert K. *Servant Leadership: A Journey into the Nature of Legitimate Power and Greatness.* Mahwah, NJ: Paulist Press, 1977.

Haughton, Rosemary. *The Transformation of Man.* Springfield, IL: Templegate Publishers, 1980.

Kasper, Cardinal Walter. *Leadership in the Church: How Traditional Roles Can Serve the Christian Community Today.* Trans. Brian McNeil. New York: Crossroad, 2003.

Mallon, James. *Divine Renovation: Bringing Your Parish from Maintenance to Mission.* New London, CN: Twenty-Third Publications, 2014.

Nouwen, Henri with Michael J. Christensen and Rebecca J. Laird. *Discernment: Reading the Signs of Daily Life.* New York: HarperOne. 2015.

Sofield, Loughlan, ST, and Carroll Juliano, SCHJ. *Collaboration: Uniting Our Gifts in Ministry*. Notre Dame, IN: Ave Maria Press, 2000.

Sofield, Loughlan, ST, and Donald H. Kuhn. *The Collaborative Leader: Listening to the Wisdom of God's People*. Notre Dame, IN: Ave Maria Press, 1995.

Steffen, Donna, SC. *Discerning Disciples: Listening for God's Voice in Christian Initiation*. Rev. ed. Chicago: Liturgy Training Publications, 2007.

Weddell, Sherry. *Forming Intentional Disciples: The Path to Knowing and Following Jesus*. Huntington, IN: Our Sunday Visitor, 2012.

———. *Becoming a Parish of Intentional Disciples*. Huntington, IN: Our Sunday Visitor, 2105.

White, Michael and Tom Corcoran. *Rebuilt: Awakening the Faithful, Reaching the Lost, and Making Church Matter*. Notre Dame, IN: Ave Maria Press. 2013.

———. *Rebuilding Your Message: Practical Tools to Strengthen Your Preaching and Teaching*. Notre Dame, IN: Maria Press, 2015.

———. *The Rebuilt Field Guide: Ten Steps for Getting Started*. Notre Dame, IN: Ave Maria Press, 2016.

———. *Tools for Rebuilding: 75 Really, Really Practical Ways to Make Your Parish Better*. Notre Dame, IN: Ave Maria Press, 2013.

Index